FRONTISPIECE (PLATE 6) White irises, dogwood, yellow pond-lilies, and, in the background, full-blown magnolias with centers surrounded by dark false ceriths. Fine plastic fern is used for foliage. The container is a pale gray porcelain vase.

Shell Art

A HANDBOOK FOR MAKING
SHELL FLOWERS, MOSAICS, JEWELRY,
AND OTHER ORNAMENTS

Helen K. Krauss

DOVER PUBLICATIONS, INC.
NEW YORK

To my dear friend, Bess Shippy,

a partner in many horticultural projects

and in sailing the seas and

roaming the beaches for sea shells

Published in Canada by General Publishing
Company, Ltd., 30 Lesmill Road, Don Mills,
Toronto, Ontario.

Published in the United Kingdom by Constable
and Company, Ltd., 10 Orange Street, London
WC 2.

This Dover edition, first published in 1976, is a
republication of the work first published in 1965.
It is reprinted by special arrangement with Hearth-
side Press, Incorporated, Publishers, 445 Northern
Boulevard, Great Neck, N.Y. 11021, publisher of
the original edition. Chapter 16 has been written
especially for the Dover edition. The list of commercial sources of shells and supplies that appeared
in the original edition is here omitted.

International Standard Book Number: 0-486-23255-7
Library of Congress Catalog Card Number:75-21356

Manufactured in the United States of America
Dover Publications, Inc.
180 Varick Street
New York, N.Y. 10014

CONTENTS

FOREWORD

Seldom does a gentle pursuit combine so many diverse talents, interests and rewarding opportunities as does the making of floral arrangements and seascapes from natural shells. The recipe for this enchanting occupation calls for a liberal share of artistry and handicraft, a blending of a knowledge of horticulture and floral arranging, a pinch of science, and a basketful of shell collecting—all steeped together in many pleasant and satisfying hours of preparation and creation.

If the decorative arts, beachcombing, and floral arranging, all have appeals of their own, imagine what a combination of all these pastimes must have to offer! This book covers all that, and is unique in representing the naturalistic school of shell arrangers who abhor artificially and gaudily dyed specimens and frown upon botanically impossible creations. The discipline of correctness results in unusually pleasing and natural arrangements which stand the test of time and fashion. The authoress qualifies in both the fields of horticulture and conchological arrangements, and adds her instinctive good taste and artistic abilities to produce a meaningful manual of instruction for shell arranging.

R. Tucker Abbott, Ph.D.
Academy of Natural Sciences
of Philadelphia

INTRODUCTION

The current revival of interest in the Victorian art of making flowers of natural-colored sea shells has inspired the writing of this book. These nineteenth-century flowers were constructed with great care and closely resembled their terrestrial counterparts. Shell bouquets typical of that era can sometimes be seen in museums or in the homes of private collectors. On rare occasions, a bouquet or matching pair of bouquets is offered for sale.

Waterproof materials were unknown when these flowers were made. The leaves and stamens were made of cotton or silk and the stalks of thin uncoated wire. Usually all of the flowers were bound to a central stem, a cylindrical length of wood. Such bouquets were always protected by glass to prevent the disintegration of fabrics, the rusting of wires, and the accumulation of dust which could not be washed away.

Rounded domes of various sizes and shapes were generally used to protect the flowers, but in France rectangular glass cases were also constructed. Some of these were richly decorated at the sides, around the base, and at the top with ormolu, a kind of brass made to resemble gold. Glass protection limited the types of flower arrangement that could be made, but because of it many of the Victorian shell bouquets have survived in good condition.

Water-glass and lacquer were used in the first attempts to waterproof silk and cotton leaves. Neither was successful. Later, the use of dyed fish scales in costume jewelry sparked the idea of making foliage sprays of green-dyed scales. Although limited in size and shape, these proved to be adequate and interesting, and they could be made impervious to water.

Today we have at our disposal an array of materials that would have astonished and delighted the craftsman of 100 years ago. Many of the new materials are waterproof and others can be made so by coatings that are easily applied. Important among them is plastic foliage, which during the past few years has been manufactured in great variety for all kinds of artificial flower arrangements. Being washable, it is eminently suitable for shell bouquets. Plastic fern leaves can be snipped apart to make small sprays, and large leaves can be cut into desired shapes.

In addition to these aids, more species of shells, and more colorful ones, have been made available to the craftsman by extended trade lines. It is now possible to make at least 130 accurate replicas of natural flowers of countless colors, and to compose any style of arrangement that can be anchored permanently in a container.

While many attractive shells can be purchased in specialty shops, the craftsman who seeks a great variety of color and form will gather them at the water's edge wherever he goes, especially on beaches in warm climates. Some very desirable shells are too delicate to be handled commercially.

When shells are used in their natural colors, nature's designs, markings, sculpturing, and blending of colors become a challenge to the most gifted artist. Small artificially colored shells (or seeds) are used only in the centers of flowers when no shell of natural color or form can be found to complete the flower artistically.

One need not be a botanist to make facsimiles of living flowers. There are lavishly illustrated botanical and horticultural books, as well as gardening magazines and catalogues, that portray flowers in all their detail. An acquaintance with these, if not with the living plants, is essential for anyone who wishes to copy flowers realistically with shells.

Accuracy of detail is of course desirable, but because shells are not flexible some concessions are made in constructing flowers. Spurs such as are found on delphinium, larkspur, and columbine are omitted. When looking at live flowers of this type, one sees very few of the spurs except in loose-flowered columbine. Their inclusion would either clutter the bouquet unnecessarily or spread the flowers so far apart that the arrangement would be ungainly. For the same reason, a compromise must sometimes be made as to the number of petals used in different flowers. The goal is to achieve a reasonable facsimile than can be easily recognized.

When gardeners or shell collectors do not know the common or technical name of a flower or sea shell, they often invent a name. This practice causes confusion. To aid in the identification of shells and flowers mentioned in these pages, a list of common or commercial names, accompanied by scientific names, is included in the index. Descriptions of the various flowers are given with as little technical terminology as possible.

ACKNOWLEDGEMENTS

Many scientific writers have contributed to the opening chapter, "The Story of Sea Shells." To each and every one, including those whose names are unknown to me, such as the anonymous writers on heraldry, I am deeply indebted.

I wish especially to thank Dr. R. Tucker Abbott, malacologist of The Academy of Natural Sciences in Philadelphia, for assistance in identifying shells known in the trade only by their common names. In addition to putting at my disposal numerous reference books and monographs on shells, he allowed me to use the Academy's collection for comparative study.

I am also particularly grateful to Gladys York Christensen for her drawings of basic flower forms, and to Bill Harris for the perfection of his photography.

PLATE 1 A Southern magnolia made of Macoma clam shells 1⅞ by 3 inches in size, arranged in a pedestaled vase covered with a rosette of large plastic leaves. In the center of the flower is a yellow African patella with black stripes that suggest stamens. Yellow-white conch shells are wired and used as buds.

PLATE 2 Red seaweed from Coronado, California, red organ coral from Australia, and Lower California and New Jersey flora and fauna enhance three Japanese shells, a South African star patella, and a Florida tulip mussel. Curled through the center is a young whelk egg case.

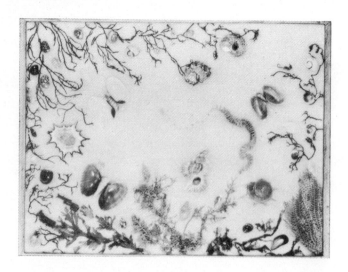

PLATE 3 An underwater garden includes Lower California, Florida, and New Jersey flora and fauna, a green clam from China, two green tusk shells from Japan, gooseneck barnacles from Mexico and New Jersey, blue mussels, razor clams, Florida chitons, shoe-button snails, a pair of pale green iridescent paper mussels, and a small multi-armed starfish from Mexico.

PLATE 4 This underwater garden has sections of a Mexican yellow multiple sea fan with tiny red spots. At the lower left are small pieces of sargassum. Shells in flower spikes include tellins and orange lucinas from Mexico; cross-barred Venus, coquinas, and Morton's cockles from Florida; and zebra shells and blue-gray snails from the West Indies. Larger shells are from Japan and Mexico.

PLATE 5 A flower arrangement in a shallow shadow box. At the top and sides are buddleijas and sprays of bell-type flowers. Other flowers include roses, daisies, miniature irises, pink clover, and a cluster of white orchids at the lower right. The leaves are made of carp scales.

PLATE 6 See frontispiece.

PLATE 7 An old-fashioned round bouquet of many bright-colored flowers. The base of the arrangement is fringed with maidenhair fern made of bonefish scales. Among the flowers are foliage sprays of carp scales.

1 THE STORY OF SEA SHELLS

Shells are the coverings of a class of animals that have inhabited our lakes and seas for millions of years. They are hardened, calcified cases which protect the fragile marine creatures within from injury and the attacks of enemies. Paleontologists have found fossil shells that date to the Paleozoic, more than 300,000,000 years ago. Primitive man, when he appeared, learned to use the animals as food and the shells as implements. Very early he seemed sensitive to the beauty of sea shells.

The shells of many marine animals have retained the same form through aeons of time. When, in recent years, southern Florida canals were deepened, and the excavated sand, marl, and fossil shells were heaped along the banks, many of the shells exposed were seen to be like those we find alive today. They had been well preserved since the Pliocene, when modern forms began to appear. Some were marked with intricate sculpture or other deviations that differentiated them from our modern shells. One species, now extinct in Florida, closely resembled the Hercules club which is abundant in Australia, where it is also known as a mud whelk.

Some animals from the Atlantic Ocean apparently found their way to the Pacific through the water that once separated North and South America. The shell animals that multiplied in the Pacific developed slightly different characters from those that remained in the Gulf of Mexico and the Caribbean Sea.

Probably the oldest find associating man with shells was a discovery in 1895. A red helmet shell and cowries from the Indian Ocean were found with the remains of a Cro-Magnon man in a cave near Dordogne, France. Cowries are the most widely known of all shells. They have also been found with bronze and iron implements and other antiquities in Transcaucasian and European graves, and in ancient Egyptian tombs.

As late as the seventeenth and eighteenth centuries, slave traders of the Guinea Coast used cowries as money, but later English gold and American dollars replaced them. After that, the shells were used for ornamental and other purposes. In some countries they can still be seen attached to the trappings of camels, horses, and other animals—presumably as a protection against the evil eye. Occasionally long strings of them are worn as beads by gypsy women.

One of the most important shells in ancient days was the murex. The creature that inhabited it secreted the material used by the Phoenicians for their famous Tyrian purple dye, said to have been worth its weight in gold. Its color was not the purple we visualize today, but more nearly red. In the Bible, red, purple, or blue dye is mentioned numerous times in the book of Exodus (Chapters 25-28 and 35-39) as having been given to the priests for robes, vestments, and curtains for the tabernacle. The colors are mentioned again in the Gospel of St. Luke (Chapter 16:9) and in The Acts (Chapter 16:14).

Dye from a similar species was made in Crete about 1600 B.C., and the Cretan dye industry extended to Cadiz, Spain. The early Romans and Egyptians used the dye in cosmetics such as eye shadow and rouge as well as for coloring cloth. To distinguish the ship of Mark Antony and Cleopatra from the rest of the Egyptian fleet, its sails were dyed solidly in Tyrian purple. The color varied considerably from dull red to magenta and a purplish blue. The royal robes of patrons limned by Renaissance artists are red, but the color was called royal purple.

The Thais shell was another source of purple dye, used by the Celts of England and by the lake dwellers of Ireland around 1000 B.C. *Purpura patula pansa*, still another shell animal, was used in prehistoric times on the northwest coast of South America and on the west coast of Central America for making purple dye. Even today the Tehuantepec Indians of Mexico make a purple dye from a *Purpura* species for dyeing cotton thread. Their conservation methods are astonishingly modern and assure them a continuous supply. After squeezing the purple juice from the animal, the Indians return it to its native habitat and let it remain there until it has secreted more purple juice for subsequent use.

Scallop shells were known to primitive man in many parts of the world. The numerous species differ in size, sculpture, texture, and color, but all have the same familiar form. In ancient Greek and Roman times the scallop shell became a symbol and motifs of it are seen in architecture and sculpture. It was also an attribute of Aphrodite who, according to legend, was foam-born of the sea.

Books on heraldry tell us that crusaders wore a scallop shell on their hats or hoods when going to or from Jerusalem. The Jacob's scallop was of such distinguished character that Pope Alexander IV decreed that it could be bought only in Compostella, Spain, and that only pilgrims of noble birth could wear it. All others had to use a cross similar to the one borne on the standard of their leader. The number of scallops or crosses on an English coat of arms tells how many members of the family took part in the crusades.

When Pompeii, destroyed by an eruption of Mount Vesuvius in 79 A.D., was unearthed by archaeologists during the nineteenth century, a Jacob's scallop, a textile cone, a pearl oyster from the Indian Ocean, and cowries were found. Dr. R. Tucker Abbott believes that Pompeii may have had a natural history museum. The Roman naturalist Pliny the Elder, who lived from 23 to 79 A.D., meeting his end during the disaster that overtook Pompeii, was the first to decribe the jet-like propulsion of the scallop swimming below and along the surface of the water.

The scallop shell has long been the symbol of the Shell Oil Company and is very familiar to motorists who see it displayed at all Shell gas stations. Before being engaged in the oil business, this company transported shells for commercial use and also as ballast. It was during this period that English shell art developed. Small shells were sought for making bouquets and mosaic-like pictures, and for ornamenting boxes.

But even before the Victorian period, shells were being used in various ways in England and France. They were often embedded along with minerals in wet plaster to decorate rooms, and there was quite a vogue for creating shell grottoes in caves, underground apartments, and rooms. Baths and marble seats were entirely encrusted with shells and minerals in many of the great houses of England.

In France rococo shell work was popular during the first half of the eighteenth century. Wall decorations composed of shells were often elaborate and executed with great delicacy. Especially popular was a motif of flower garlands around the wall at the ceiling line, and shell mosaic walls encrusted with shell flowers were often works of art. Included with petaled flowers were univalves that suggested large buds and partially opened lilies.

Vases and urns to hold bouquets of shell flowers were either carved from wood or made of ceramics. Those of ceramics were often encrusted with small shells. Good examples of these bouquets may sometimes be seen in private American collections, and occasionally a soiled and faded one is offered in an antique or thrift shop or at a rummage sale. Collectors usually buy them at a low price, remove the faded fabric foliage, clean the flowers, sometimes add others, and substitute new shells for broken ones. The Victorian period piece then becomes an up-to-date ornament. Encrusted urns can be similarly restored by washing thoroughly and replacing missing shells.

At a later date small tables were ornamented with shell mosaics, and finials for lamps were made of shells simulating ceramic flowers. The glass holders of hurricane lamps too were often twined with shell flowers.

Necklaces, bracelets, and earrings were fashioned of shells in ancient times and the wearing of such ornaments has continued to our day. Shell flower ornaments made of cut or sliced shells are now much in vogue. When shells are cut, the brilliant interior colors of univalves are revealed, which otherwise are not seen. Diamond saws, used for slicing shells today, were not available to the Spaniards who conquered Mexico. Nevertheless, they carved thin slices from coral-colored shells as trinkets to give the Indians.

So the shell trade has continued to our century and is a large and important industry today, serving button factories, collectors, and wholesale and retail jewelry makers.

2 COLLECTING SHELLS

Walking the beaches is the usual procedure in shell collecting. Make sure that the specimens you gather are not pitted, worn, faded, or coated with calcareous matter (deposits of lime). Most shells look bright when water from recent waves is still on them, but careful examination often reveals imperfections. When they are absolutely dry, even the casual collector will notice the blemishes. Damaged shells cannot be restored to their natural beauty; broken pieces, however, can sometimes be used for small flower parts.

In calm weather, shells in good condition are most likely to be found along the different tide lines from the water's edge to the upper reaches of the previous high-tide line. After a storm, one can walk well beyond the recent high-tide line and find shells, some of which may still contain live animals. On more or less uninhabited and unfrequented beaches, little shells are often found piled in ridges a foot or more high. At these places one may sit and gather a pint of small shells in a reasonably short time.

Live shells are often collected in shallow water by divers equipped with face masks and snorkels, and good dead shells are also located in this way. In clear water they are gathered by deep sea divers at depths of twenty feet or more. Those from deeper waters differ from the ones found in shallows. Some species are clothed tightly with a coarse mossy substance and are scarcely recognizable by novice collectors. Others are covered with the mantles (folds of the body wall) of their respective animals, which withdraw into their shells when alarmed, revealing a clean surface.

Collectors of miniature shells use a fine sieve or screen. Buckets of sand, marl, or a combination of both, are taken from shallow water or from piled-up dredgings from deeper locations. This material is sifted at leisure through fine-meshed screens. If it becomes lumpy and dry, the lumps can be moistened with water containing a very small amount of chlorine bleach (household bleach). This softens them so that they can be fingered without crushing the small delicate shells. If large quantities of sand and marl are to be searched, a large box with a fine screen is often used.

Dedicated collectors know that shells can be found in places other than seashores and marine waters. They look for them also in secluded back bays, along the margins of freshwater lakes and rivers, and gather them at low tide from rocks and the sheltered nooks beneath them, and from grasses, shrubs and trees along the water's edge.

Interesting small shells are often found attached to larger ones. After storms, when the waves have tossed seaweed, sea fans and other coral to the high-tide lines, many precious shells can be found clinging to them. During especially violent storms, shells are even tossed into low trees *above* the high-tide line.

PRECAUTIONS WHEN SHELL-HUNTING

In collecting shells, remember that unnecessary destruction of animal life is not to be condoned. Gathering empty shells is preferable to collecting live ones, and empty ones are plentiful at times, especially after storms. Thoughtless, selfish collectors are known to have completely stripped beds of certain species only to throw away the surplus later when the animals were half dead and far from their natural habitat. Another kind of inconsiderate collector combs the beach with a coarse rake, hunting large shells, and by this method breaks up smaller precious ones sought by others.

When looking for shells, take only what you need. Do not destroy what others could use. And if, in your search, you overturn rocks which shelter these delicate sea creatures, replace them in their normal position after shells have been gathered so that the habitat will be preserved.

WHAT TO LOOK FOR

The shells that we seek for flower-making vary as flowers vary. They may be large or small, thick and heavy or so thin that they are translucent. This thickness or thinness is characteristic of both univalves and bivalves, the two main types of shells. A univalve has a single shell and a hornlike plate called an *operculum* which serves as a trapdoor when the animal withdraws into its house and as a foot when it emerges and crawls along the surface of sand or mud. These valves open and close. More than two-thirds of all known shells are univalves. A bivalve, such as the clam, has two similar parts, called valves, that are hinged together.

Bivalves are principally used for flower making. Their various sizes and colors make them useful as petals; some of the very small ones are used as flower centers. But univalves are also needed, especially to simulate individual buds or, in groups, to be placed at the tips of panicles and spikes of flowers such as lilacs and larkspurs. Univalves about two inches long can represent buds of fairly large flowers. Half-inch ones accompany flowers that are proportionately smaller, or can be fashioned into tall simple panicles. Small univalves, less than a half-inch long, belong in the more delicate sprays. Two species of rice shells are valuable for making daisies, and white Chinese slippers of different sizes and contorted shapes can be used effectively in making the type of gardenia or camellia that has reflexed petals.

WHERE TO SEARCH

The warm waters of tropical and subtropical regions—and of cold regions that are warmed by ocean rivers such as the Gulf

Stream and the Japan Current—yield the most brilliantly colored shells. The Great Barrier Reef in Australia produces the largest that is known, the giant white clam. It often measures more than two feet across, and has coarse sawtooth edges. A single valve may weigh more than two hundred pounds. Large ones are used as bird baths and smaller ones as planters and containers. At the other end of the scale are mature shells that measure less than one-eighth of an inch.

Some shells are world-wide in distribution. Among these are the scallop and its relatives; the limpet and patella group, and snails. Fully grown shells of the first group range from five-eighths of an inch to ten inches in size, and vary in sculpture and color according to species and habitat. Cupped valves of the largest ones are used for baking dishes, smaller ones go into collectors' boxes, and those that are extremely delicate are displayed in glass-covered frames. In between are shells of sizes suitable for the making of flowers and other ornaments.

Limpets and patellas live on water-washed rocks along desolate shores. Their color range is extensive. Most of them are oval in outline, though some appear distorted and a few are sharply pointed. Some are deeply cupped. The rims of different species may be smooth or slightly ruffled. The keyhole limpet has an opening in the center. Forms and colors of a species are likely to vary in different habitats.

Snails seem to lead a sort of double life. Those that like a watery location live on rocks that are washed by the waves at high tide. Often they ascend trees and return later to their wet rocks. Genuine tree snails are terrestrial animals and live entirely in trees. The most colorful snails are the one-inch Cuban tree snails (*Polymita picta*) with decorative motifs on a white, yellow, orange, or bright-brown background, and the New Guinea tree snail (*Papuina*) which is grass-green, a rare color in shells.

FLORIDA SEA SHELLS

Fortunate indeed is the zealous collector who can travel to distant shores in search of rare and beautiful shells. However, the beaches of our own country yield a rich harvest, and it is always possible to buy some of the exotic shells from dealers.

If you go to Florida on a vacation—or if you live there—visit some of the less frequented shores for shell gathering. On rocks in the Florida Keys numerous small and colorful univalves with intricate designs can be collected. There and elsewhere you may find some of the following useful forms:

SNAILS. Small snails which can be used as the centers of flowers are found washed up on the beaches and stranded, or they can be collected alive. Rock snails of various sculptured forms can be located at low tide. Small shells can be bought in local shops, of course, but these have often been bleached to such an extent that their colorful markings have disappeared completely.

BARNACLES. Dead white barnacles are used for lilies-of-the-valley. They are of various sizes and are found washed ashore on sandy beaches or attached to dead pen-shells. They may also be taken from the upper branches of mangrove trees growing along margins of waterways in the Gulf of Mexico region, Caribbean sea and inlets on the Florida coast. Live ones with lavender stripes or streaks are seen attached to the lower branches and are sometimes found washed ashore from rocks after a storm.

CHITONS. The eight transverse plates which characterize chitons have many uses in flower making. Live specimens of these small mollusks can be found on rocks at low tide in the lower Florida Keys and also on the shores of West Indian islands. Where they are abundant, they can be selected for size. The upper sides of the valves are inconspicuous and, to the inexperienced collector, appear to be part of the rock. The interior of the valves is black and blue and the hinge teeth are light blue. The two rounded end segments are particularly desirable for the centers of small flowers.

To remove chitons from the rocks to which they cling so tenaciously, use a spatula or a long flat knife. The animals can easily be extracted from their shells (see page 33).

Pink chiton segments, shaded or streaked with salmon-pink or blue, can be bought in shell shops. Most of these are large and more suitable for making jewelry. Smaller ones are available for flowers, but they must be selected carefully.

LIMPETS. Limpets are inconspicuous little shells that cling to rocks at the shoreline. In shape they are like diminutive Chinese hats of traditional style. They can be easily removed at low tide.

DENTALIUMS.   Dentaliums, which are tube-shaped, are often called tooth shells. Live white ones with pinkish tips have been found at low tide at the water's edge. The perfect shells are too long for most flowers, but broken ones can be collected along the different tide lines for use as stamens.

MUSSELS.   Mussels are bound to rocks and other surfaces by filaments known as *byssuses,* which they secrete. Hooked mussels, because of their curved outline, are useful for flower petals. They are found growing at the roots of mangrove trees with oysters as companions, and are plentiful in the general area of Bonita Springs. The inside of each valve is an iridescent reddish-purple color with white or cream-colored margins.

SCALLOPS.   Scallop shells of several kinds are plentiful on the west coast of Florida, among them the calico scallop, found principally toward the south. In their adult stage, calico scallops are from one to two inches across. After a storm or strong tide, many hundreds are washed ashore alive and trapped temporarily in lagoons. At such time the collector can gather what he needs; otherwise only single valves are found. Bay scallops from the same general area are bone-white and larger.

OLIVES.   Olives crawl on the surface of the sand at night and are frequently gathered with the aid of a strong flashlight. If they are slightly below the surface in the early morning or at dusk when the tide is low, their tracks are visible and they are easily dug out.

COCKLES.   Egg cockles, marked with yellow, white, and lavender, are found on the Florida Keys. They are just the right shape for making tulips. Morton's cockles are found at low tide on sandy and marl flats.

CLAMS.   On an unhabited outer island of the Florida Keys, macoma clam shells have been collected. Because they are abruptly bent at one end, they are perfect for making magnolia flowers. Rose-petal clams can be gathered on sandy or marl flats at low tide from Sanibel Island southward on the bay side, and around Marco Island.

TELLINS.   White tellins are found in the same area as clams. There are also a few places on the mainland where they are washed up on the beaches. Sometimes the rarer yellow- and orange-blotched ones are found with them. A longer tellin, colored pink and known as the Bahama rose-petal, is useful for making good-sized dahlias and other flowers of similar size. These shells are sometimes mottled with gray.

COQUINAS. There are many coquina species, distributed throughout the Americas and elsewhere, but the ones most desirable for flower-making are found on the sandy beaches of southwest Florida. Collecting live ones provides considerable amusement. At low tide, when each succeeding wave reaches farther up on the beach, the many-colored little animals are washed out of the sand but they burrow back into it faster than they can be grabbed by human hands. A receding tide also washes them out. Sifting the sand with a wire-mesh screen is the best way to collect them in any quantity. When the valves are opened they resemble a butterfly's wings, and coquinas are often collected for the colorful patterns on the outside of their shells. For flowers, however, the inner side is exposed.

LUCINAS. Shells of lucinas are roundish, mostly smooth, and nearly white. Some are only a quarter-inch across, others two inches or more. Several species of lucina are used for making different kinds of flowers. The cross-hatched and Pennsylvania lucinas are found on the Keys and the Florida lucina is abundant in shallow waters from Tampa southward. The buttercup lucina, one of the larger ones, has a circular band of yellow or orange. Those with the best colors are found on Sanibel Island. All sizes are useful in making different kinds of flowers.

GULF OF MEXICO

West of Florida, in the back bay waters of Mustang Island on the gulf coast of Texas, a pinkish lavender clam is found which is known locally as a lavender Venus. It is about the same size as the pointed Venus but is broader in the middle and the points are variable. The shells of some have a dark eye in the center of each valve; others have a margin in a deeper shade of lavender.

Cozumel Island, off the coast of Yucatán, yields many interesting species. In 1962, Mrs. R. Tucker Abbott and I went there to collect shells for the Malacological Department of the Philadelphia Academy of Sciences. We found ninety species, but I shall briefly mention only a few of them. On the rocky coast by the road we found a number of rock dwellers. These included the handsome prickly winkle (*Tectarius tunicatus*) with conspicuous white knobs, some shaped like tiaras; gray-blue periwinkles that are smoother but finely sculptured; red keyhole limpets, and several species of chiton.

Divers brought up large conchs (*Strombus* species) with blended orange and yellow lips, some flushed with pink; king and queen helmets (*Cassis* species), and one large chank-shell (*Xancus* species). While diving, Mrs. Abbott collected live flamingo tongues a little over an inch long. Their beautiful mantles were still visible when she brought them out of the water. Two long stretches of sandy beach are reached by boat. On them we found orange-rimmed lucinas, some rare large marginellas (*Prunum labiatum*) and other interesting shells.

PACIFIC COAST

Beaches on Puget Sound in Washington are fruitful hunting grounds for shells. Those found there include a white and yellow Thais (*Thais lamellosa*) with rows of narrow ruffles extending up and down them, pink scallops two inches or more across (*Chlamys hastatus hericus*), and light yellow scallops.

From the Pacific side of the state of Washington come shells in pink, soft yellow, white, and purple-shaded, chiefly *Tellina salmonea* and *Tellina philippinarum* (this the purple one). All are useful in making pansies.

On the Pacific side of La Paz in Lower California, shells shaped somewhat like tellinas have been found, a species known to malacologists as *Heterodonax bimaculata*. They are white, or sometimes dusty pink, with short dark stripes radiating to the margin. Some have a dark blotch near the hinge. Another shell is a lucina species, small and of a soft orange color.

THE WEST INDIES

The islands of the Caribbean have a wealth of sea shells. Endemic to Grand Cayman are two-inch green and black turbos and wide-mouthed purpuras (*Purpura patula*), found living on rocks. Zebra shells *(Purperita pupa)* can be gathered in tidal pools, and on unfrequented beaches emerald nerites can be collected.

Emerald nerites were also gathered on a sandy beach near San Juan in Puerto Rico by sifting handfuls of sand through the fingers. At a remote pebbly beach reached by boat, innumerable colorful and variously shaped limpets were collected. Other small shells such as the Hungarian hat were among them. These are white shells with deep pink or rose streaks or blotches. Others in the group have a deep purple blotch. All are about a half inch in size.

At the Estero, about ten miles south of San Salvador, several specimens of generally unknown shells have been collected. Included among them were white boat-shells with a conspicuous yellow spot at the point, elongated narrow coquinas, large blood-red tellins, white cuplike shells of small to medium size which are probably a kind of cockle, and angled pink shells shaded with violet in small to medium sizes.

On a sandy western beach of Eleuthera in the Bahama group, I have collected many small scallops (*Chlamys benedicti*). They ranged in color through various shades of yellow to a light soft orange. Another species, which is less fragile and more cupped, has a large russet blotch at the hinge. Various other kinds of *Chlamys* have been found on this beach, some sculptured and flecked with minute short streaks. Perfect pairs are almost impossible to obtain, but single valves can often be matched for making flowers.

Bermuda is rich in shell fauna and the best time for collecting there is during the summer months. Areas suitable for combing include gravelly beaches. Those on the south side have gaudy asaphis shells (*Asaphis deflorata*); those on the north have numerous rock species. Pink Beach, named for its pink sand, has an abundance of tiny pink shells (*Synaptocochlea picta*) that are interesting and unusual. Other shells also drift onto the beach. In the sand on the west side of King's Point lives *Heterodonax bimaculata*, which is larger than the Mexican tellin found at La Paz in Lower California.

HAWAIIAN ISLANDS

Most tourists to the Hawaiian area go to Oahu, where the city of Honolulu stands. Offhand consideration would suggest that innumerable fascinating shells could be gathered on the sub-tropical beaches there, but actually three-quarters of the island's shore line is battered by waves strong enough to smash drifting shells to bits. If you can dive, or get someone to dive for you, you may make some interesting finds such as various large cones.

Shell hunting is better on the island of Hawaii, a short distance from Oahu by airplane. On a visit there we made Kona our headquarters and drove around the coast. We found a number of white-sand beaches and stopped at one where outdoor cooking facilities were available. Around us on the sand we found conspicuous white drupas about an inch across that were decorated with an orderly arrangement of raised black dots. On nearby rocks we found several species of *Patella*; others lay on the sand. The most unusual one was slightly more than an inch and a quarter across and was the largest of its kind that we found. The cup side of this shell is a pearly translucent white and the outer surface has closely set raised black radial lines, and many very narrow white lines depressed between the black ones. Other patellas, small choice forms, measured about half an inch across and had rippled edges.

FRANCE

Shells of many species are washed ashore on both the Atlantic and Mediterranean coasts of France, and along the margins of her bays, gulfs, and inlets. Some species are found only on the Atlantic side, others only along the Mediterranean, but usually the species of a family are distributed throughout the area.

Peculiar to the Bay of Biscay side are bright-yellow, orange, and brownish-tan snails (*Littorina obtusa*) up to a half-inch in size, and abundantly distributed; bubble-shells (*Bulla*), one species of which is shaped somewhat like a cornet; spindle shells (*Fusus rostratus*) with long canals; purple-blotched coquinas (*Donax anatium*); winged oysters (*Avicula hirunda*) with nacreous interiors, and two species of *Murex*. One species (*Murex brandaris*) has a long tail; the other (*Murex trunculus*) has a short broad canal from which the ancients extracted royal-purple dye.

Common to both areas are brownish-tan turret shells (*Turitella communis*) up to two and a quarter inches long with ropelike whorls from tip to base; pale-violet precious wentle-traps (*Scala communis*); scallop shells (*Pecten* and *Chlamys* species); top shells (several *Caliostoma* species); cockles, including several *Cardium* species; and Hungarian hats (*Capulus hungarius*) with a white interior and a brown exterior that suggests stocking caps with tapering ends that curl forward. The most colorful shells found on the coasts of France are small tellins (*Tellina tenuis*) of many apricot and blended pink shades. But these are thin and transparent—more suitable for a collection than for flowers. They measure about an inch across. Another handsome shell that is found on French shores is the Pandora (*Pandora inequivalvis*), an inch or more long. The interior of the valves is pearly, and one valve is flatter than the other. This shell is abundant on many sandy beaches. Many species in addition to these are collected by shellers, including the edible piddock (*Pholas dactylus*), which sometimes resembles a medium-sized angel's wing.

FROM OTHER DISTANT SHORES

Some of the lovely shells from distant shores can be purchased from commercial dealers, but many of them are rarely collected and therefore scarce. You either collect them during your travels or trade them with friends who know private collectors in remote places. I know of no dealers in New Zealand, but by trading rare shells from my own collection I have been able to obtain beautiful orange-red lamp shells and ruffled jingle shells. The goal is to make flowers of as many forms and colors as possible, hence our interest in exotic species. There is no better inspiration than that provided by an extensive and varied collection of beautiful shells.

Among interesting ones are Japanese scallops, varying in size from one and a half to three inches, with the paired shells matching in color. One of the unusual and distinctive colors in which they are available is a deep violet. A smaller species is yellow, sometimes blotched with light brown. This is excellent for making a poppy with crinkled petals.

From South Africa and New Zealand come small scallops of many colors, some in red and other brilliant hues. These are so delicate that flowers made with them must be constructed directly on a board or panel. Once they are glued they cannot be removed without being broken.

Another interesting and useful shell, which can be found in shell shops, is that of the Philippine window oyster. This is a white translucent shell which has been used for many years as a substitute for glass in windows and doors. In Hawaii, such leaded squares are sold in panels for making lamp shades and screens. Lingerie boxes with tops made of whole shells welded together in flat sheets have also been seen. Such shells can be used to decorate glass or plastic screen panels. Dyed green, they can be used effectively to represent the leaves of water-lilies.

PLATE 8 OPPOSITE BELOW Sprays of white dogwood and early-flowering, full-blown magnolias; one small spray of tarpon scale flowers, and a large white iris in the center of the arrangement. Since the flowers appear before the leaves, the stems are wrapped with brown. Buds are represented by small fluted conch shells. The base is a piece of Florida driftwood.

3 PREPARING THE SHELLS

Whether the shells you plan to use have been hand-gathered or purchased in a shop, they should be washed thoroughly before flowers are made. Use warm soapy water and a soft cloth or brush, then rinse them in clear water.

The apertures of rice-shells may be filled with hardened marl, shell fragments, and other debris. All such extraneous matter should be removed so that the rolled lips of the shells suggest the curled appearance of certain daisy rays.

BLEACHING

Some small shells sold commercially have already been bleached. Those that have not, both white and colored ones, and all dead shells that have been collected, will be more attractive if they are soaked in a solution of chlorine bleach (Clorox, Prox, or such) in water. A one-minute immersion is sufficient for delicate shells and small thin ones. Heavier and larger shells can be left in the bleach until minor blemishes have disappeared. From five minutes to more than half an hour may be required, so examine them frequently. After the bleaching process, wash them again thoroughly.

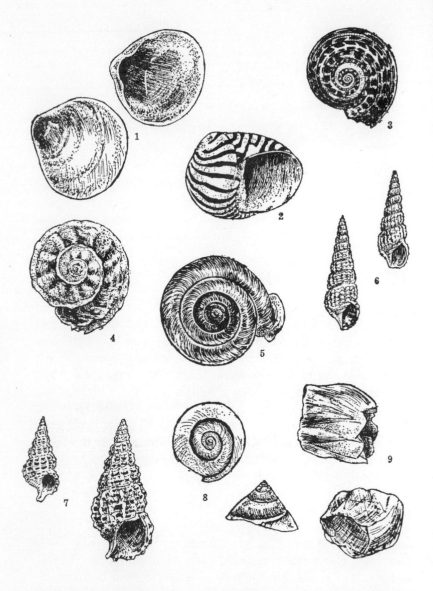

1. Small Rose Cups, to ⅜ inch; 2. Zebra Shell, to ½ inch; 3. Small Snail, to ⅜ inch; 4. Shoe-button Snail, to ½ inch; 5. Flat Coiled Snail, to ⅜ inch; 6. Slender Cerith, to ⅝ inch; 7. Fly-specked Cerith (young), to ¼ inch; 7a. Fly-specked Cerith (adult), ¾ inch; 8. Striped Olive (top cut), to ³⁄₁₆ inch; 9. Tulip Barnacle.

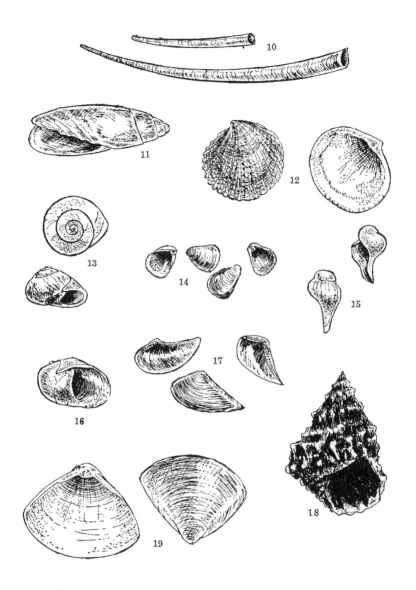

10. Tooth Shell; 11. Rice Shell, to ⅝ inch; 12. Small White Cups, from ⅛ to ¼ inch; 13. Pikaki Shell, to ⅛ inch; 14. Lilac Shells, to ³⁄₁₆ inch; 15. Young Whelks, to ⁵⁄₁₆ inch; 16. Green Snail, to ¼ inch; 17. Job's Tears, to ¼ inch; 18. False Prickly Winkle, to ½ inch or slightly more; 19. White Nut Clam, to ½ inch.

OILING

To further enhance the brightness of white as well as colored shells, rub each one with baby oil or light machine oil diluted with cigaret-lighter fluid, using two parts of oil to one of fluid. Apply the mixture to the shells with a camel's-hair artist's brush so as to get into all the crevices. Oil alone is sometimes used, but the lighter fluid makes it penetrate the shells better; also it helps to remove grease. It will then evaporate. In the process of oiling, discard any shells that are noticeably spotted with calcareous matter or tar. These substances are impossible to remove.

REMOVING SKINS

Some shells—among them the Florida tulip mussel and the Maine fresh water mussel—are covered with a horny skin called a *periostracum*. This skin can usually be removed with coarse emery cloth. If the shell is thick and the skin is tough, more drastic measures must be taken. One method recommended for removing the tough skins of shells that have glossy and colorful interiors is to soak them in a solution of water and muriatic acid. Muriatic acid is hydrochloric acid, diluted with water. It must be handled with extreme care because it can eat holes in metal pans and clothing and cause severe burns if it comes into contact with the hands.

The first step in this process is to coat the inner side of each shell with paraffin to protect it. Then select a glass or porcelain bowl to hold the acid solution.

For medium-sized shells, dilute three or four ounces of muriatic acid with one gallon of water. For large shells a stronger solution is often necessary. Small shells are easier to handle if they are placed in an improvised bag. Arrange them on a square of cheesecloth, take up the corners, and tie them securely with string. Dip the paraffin-coated shells, or the bag of shells, into the acid for a few seconds, then wash them in *cold* water to stop the action of the acid. Next wash the shells in soapy water and rinse them thoroughly.

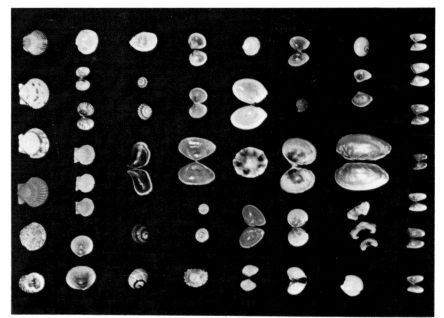

PLATE I

PLATE II

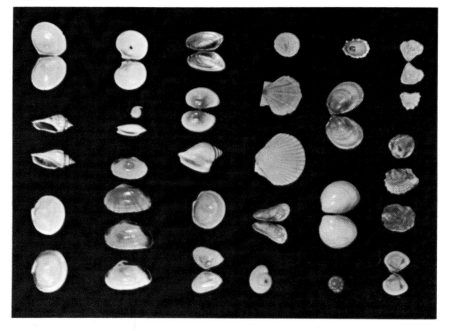

PLATE III An antiqued pink bowl filled with rose, pink, and pale salmon geraniums. Included are a small cluster of pink flowers characteristic of the scented-leaved kinds and one of the rosebud form. Drooping buds are made of matching coquina shells. Interspersed are sprays of leaves made from tarpon scales.

PLATE IV   An assortment of flowers arranged in an East Indian clam shell mounted on a head of white coral.

PLATE V   A mixed bouquet of flowers of many kinds and colors with plastic maidenhair fern. The base is an East Indian tiger clam shell, balanced with two snail shells.

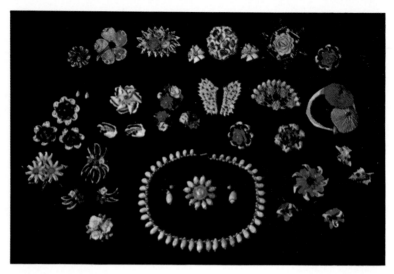

PLATE VI Shell jewelry made of natural color shells, cut shells, dyed shells and garfish scales.

PLATE VII An underwater garden of colorful coral from Lower California. Adhering to a delicate sea plant are three sections of the skeleton of a spiny sea urchin.

PLATE VIII This plate shows a fiber glass panel decorated with shells and sea animals. The most distinctive decoration is the half-section of a nautilus, showing its "pearly chambers."

PLATE IX This antique frame with convex glass contains many kinds of colorful flowers, combined with foliage made of carp scales. The oval shape of the frame makes it possible to see the flowers from a height.

PLATE X An antique brown shadow box with calla lilies made of fig shells. The petals of the white cupped flower with brown interior were cut from univalves. Brown flowers at lower right of pointed Venus shells. Leaves are of carp scales.

PLATE XI Shadow box flowers include spikes of grape hyacinths, dahlias, cherry blossoms, and a Japanese anemone. Clethras, at right, are small fly-specked ceriths.

PLATE XII A modern version of an octagonal Victorian shadow box containing mosaics and flowers.

PLATE XIII A spring bouquet of lilacs, bridal wreath, verbascum, and pop-
ies. Various kinds of plastic leaves have been used. Between the clusters of
bridal wreath are small carp scales.

PLATE XIV Bowl of pansies made from tellins with a large scallop shell for
a container.

Another method of removing the periostracum calls for chloride of lime. Make a paste of chloride of lime and water and apply it to the shells with a toothbrush. Let it remain until the skin has disappeared. Several hours' contact may be necessary for very tough skins, but a periodical inspection should be made to see how matters are progressing. If left too long, the paste may blemish the surface of the shells. When the skin has been dissolved, remove the excess lime, wash the shells in warm soapy water, and rinse them carefully.

REMOVING LIVE ANIMALS

If shells contain live animals, these must be removed. There are three ways to do it.

Method 1. Place the shells in a pan of water, bring the water to the boiling point, and then remove the pan from the fire. When the shells are cool enough to handle, put the shells in a pan of fresh water and flush the animals out of their shells. Then wash the shells in warm soapy water and rinse them well.

Method 2. Another way is to place small shells in a pan or jar of fresh water, and change the water frequently. Each time it is changed some of the dead animals will float out with the stale water. When coquinas and other bivalves of similar size are left in water overnight, the shells open and the animals can be removed easily. Again, wash and rinse the shells carefully.

Method 3. The animals of small univalves such as rice-shells and dentaliums cannot be removed easily without breaking their shells. Place them in a jar of alcohol and let them soak for two weeks.

SORTING SHELLS

When your shells have been bleached, cleaned, and oiled, sort them for color and size. Separate the shells of bivalves that are hinged on the left side from those that are hinged on the right. This makes it possible for the hinges to face in the same direction when a flower is being made.

When more or less rounded shells—such as Morton's cockles, rose cups, and lucinas—are used in constructing a flower, the hinges are either imbedded at the center of a flower or arranged at the outer edge to simulate curled petals. They need to be sorted only for color and size.

Some shell flowers are more attractive when the hinges are partly concealed by overlapping each one in turn. Valves with distinctive blotches should not be overlapped, so that a flower will show characters often seen in exotic live flowers. Sort separately shells that are to be used in this way. Among them are the pointed Venus, lavender Venus, and the gaudy asaphis.

Sorting bivalves into carefully matched pairs is not necessary for flower making. Pairs are often broken apart by the waves and washed ashore in good condition. Such valves can be matched easily with other single ones.

The important thing to remember in preparing and sorting the shells you plan to use for flower making is to discard those that are sun-bleached or scarred. Use only perfect ones for sprays and bouquets and take time to prepare them correctly.

PLATE 9   Sprays of orchid-pink clematis made of Maine fresh water mussels and white clematis made of broad California tellins. Maidenhair and asparagus plastic fern foliage complete the ensemble.

4 MATERIALS AND TOOLS

For making shell flowers you will need quite an assortment of materials and small tools. Some are purchased from shell supply companies, some from hardware stores, drugstores, and groceries (found in your yellow pages telephone directory). None is very expensive and it is best to stock them all.

From shell companies you should obtain the following items, which are used as described:

1. *Clear White Plastic Disks* from one half to two inches in diameter for use as bases in making average-sized and large flowers.

2. *Orinoco, Bond #537*, or *Shellfast* shell glue. These three brands of glue are fast drying, an advantage in making flowers, especially double ones.

3. *Green Covered Wire, #26* gauge. This wire is strung through the two holes of a disk. The ends, twisted together beneath the disk, provide an anchorage for wires used as stems.

4. *White Covered Wire.* Fine-gauge wire, covered with white, is less conspicuous for white shells that are being wired to serve as petals for large double flowers.

5. *Wired Chenille Cord*, or *Pipe Cleaners.* Some flowers are constructed within rings made of wired cord. Such rings may be of any size desired. They can be shallow, or they can be built up for the construction of unstemmed, slightly- or

deeply-cut flowers. Their function is to hold the first row of shell petals in position. Rings used in flower construction are always placed on a sheet of oiled glass or sturdy, pliable plastic when flowers are being made.

6. *Long-nosed Nippers.* These are used to straighten and bend wires, and to twist them into desired positions.

7. *Tweezers.* Select the kind that has curved serrated points. These are used to pick up small shells and place them in position when making flowers. Straight tweezers can be used, but those with serrated points are better because they hold small shells firmly. They are especially useful for arranging tiny shells to form the center of a flower.

8. *Shell Lacquer.* All dyed materials such as green covered wire, green-dyed cotton, seeds, fish scales, tiny yellow-dyed shells, and artificial daisy centers should be brushed or sprayed with shell lacquer. This seals the pores and coats the dyes so that they will not run and stain the flowers when shell bouquets are washed. All lacquers tend to yellow, but yellowing does not particularly affect the greens and browns that are generally used in bouquets.

In addition to these items, other materials are needed which are obtainable from florist shops. These are:

1. *Coated Wire.* A selection of several gauges should be made for flower stems. The pliable stems of small flowers that need to be arched or bent require firm but more pliable wire than is used for straight stems. Large or heavy shell flowers require heavy-gauge wires for their stems.

2. *Green Floratape.* Get the half-inch width and cut it lengthwise down the middle for wrapping the stems of different flowers. The narrow width makes a smoother and neater stem. Floratape is waterproof and does not need to be lacquered.

3. *Green Floral Clay.* Floral clay is usually sold in brick form and there are two types, hard and soft. The hard clay is better for shell bouquets because it holds the flowers firmly in position even when the container is inverted. Soft clay is less dependable and has the added disadvantage of becoming softer in warm weather. In either case, flowers are likely to be displaced. Floral clay is packed in the container to any desired depth and the flower stems are inserted in it.

4. *Green Styrofoam* and special *Adhesive Strips*. The Styrofoam is useful as a holder when a few sprays are used in a flower arrangement. It is not strong enough to support a large heavy bouquet. The adhesive strips are used to fasten the Styrofoam block to the container.

5. *Re-usable Plastic*. This type of plastic is used to anchor shells temporarily when designs are being plotted on panels. It enables the craftsman to move the shells from place to place until the desired effect is achieved. The plastic is then removed and the shells are glued in their permanent positions. The plastic is then stored for later use.

Other items and materials needed for making shell flowers can be bought in hardware stores or hobby shops, drugstores, and groceries. They are:

1. *Wire Shears*. Shears made for the purpose are best for cutting wire of all gauges.

2. *Small Electric Drill*. Such a drill is needed to make the two holes near the base of heavy shells by means of which they are wired to disks. When a shell has been drilled, a fine wire is strung through each hole and brought down closely over the edge. The four ends are then twisted together carefully to avoid breakage and the shell is ready to be fastened securely to a disk.

3. *Very Fine Spool Wire*. Such wire can be used to wire fish scales as well as drilled shells. It is a substitute for fine covered wire of any color. When used it should be lacquered because it is not rust-proof.

4. *Wooden Toothpicks*. These have many uses in the construction of shell flowers. They will not scratch shells when used to maneuver them into position or to press them into glue. When a spot of glue is needed to secure a shell to cotton, it can be applied neatly with a toothpick. (When glue is squeezed directly from a tube onto the base of a shell, or onto a bare spot that needs covering, too much may be applied so that other shells are coated and the resulting flower looks messy.)

5. *Absorbent Cotton*. Absorbent cotton has many uses. It is important in binding shells and disks together, and is used in molding flower spikes and ball-shaped flowers.

6. *Waxed Paper*, a *Pane of Glass*, or a thick pliable *Plastic Sheet*. When flowers are constructed individually, a working

surface of one of these materials is needed. Glue sometimes spreads beyond the thin layer of cotton that is used under the shells, forming a thin sheet. This can be cut away with small scissors. If flowers stick to waxed paper, remove them with a razor blade. Glass can be oiled to make removal easier, but any excess glue must be scraped off before additional flowers are made. No coating is needed to facilitate the removal of flowers from a plastic sheet. Should one or two appear to adhere, bending the sheet releases them. Excess glue can be brushed off.

7. *Baby Oil, Light Machine Oil or Mineral Oil.* Glass used as a work top should be oiled to facilitate the removal of flowers. A little applied to the hands makes the removal of dried glue easy. Wiping shells with oil containing a little lighter fluid enhances their color and luster. Apply the same mixture with a cotton-wrapped toothpick to any white spots that appear on shells in a bouquet.

8. *Chlorine Bleach.* This is "household bleach," readily identified by its odor, which is sold under such trade names as Clorox, Prox, and Star Water. It is used to remove minor blemishes from shells. The strength of the solution is determined by the size and thickness of the shells to be treated, and the amount of extraneous matter that must be removed (see page 29).

All implements used in constructing shell flower bouquets should be cleaned thoroughly after each use. Deposits of glue on a pane of glass should be scraped off with a razor blade. Metal tools must be cleaned; glue that adheres to them prevents them from functioning properly.

5 BASIC FORMS OF FLOWER MAKING

Nature produces flowers in a bewildering assortment of shapes and sizes and arranges them on their stems in a diversity of ways. Botanists describe their attributes precisely in a language all their own, but for our purposes we need know only enough about flower forms and inflorescences (arrangements of flowers on stems) to serve as a basis for our construction.

Some flowers are spoken of as "single," others as "double." A wild rose is called a single flower because it has only one circle of petals. A hybrid tea or other such rose that has many concentric rows of petals is said to be double. Different techniques are used in constructing single and double flowers with shells.

Certain kinds of flowers which are called single, as a daisy, are actually composed of many very tiny flowers compressed into a head with petal-like rays surrounding the central "button." Chrysanthemums and dahlias have the same basic form, but most of them have many rows of these petal-like rays, and they are then designated as double flowers. Clovers grow in another kind of compact head, one without rays. Flowering dogwood also has a number of small flowers in a compact head which is surrounded by showy, petal-like bracts. In shellwork, all heads are treated as individual flowers.

Some flowers grow singly at the end of a stem. Others grow in twos or threes, or in many-flowered clusters of various designs, such as spikes, racemes, panicles, cymes, corymbs, and umbels. These inflorescence types are classified by the arrangement of the stalks which support the flowers.

The main axis of a flower cluster, to which one or more other parts may be attached, is the *stem*, or *stalk*. The secondary stems which branch off from it are the *peduncles*. These may bear the flowers or they may give rise to finer branches, called *pedicels*, which bear the individual flowers.

When flowers are set closely against a stem, without a noticeable peduncle, the arrangement is called a *spike*. Grape hyacinth is an example, but only in part; the lower flowers may have short stalks. When stalks (peduncles) are present throughout, as in larkspur, the flowers are said to be in a *raceme*. If the flowers occur on branched stems rather than on single stalks arising from the main stem, the structure is a *panicle*.

Rounded flower clusters are designated by still other names. When all of the pedicels (or peduncles) arise from the same level around the tip of a peduncle (or stem), as in bridal-wreath, the inflorescence is an *umbel*. Some umbels are branched, or compound, as in Queen Anne's lace. A flat-topped cluster of flowers with their peduncles arranged around a stem in a close spiral is a *corymb;* the peduncles of the outer flowers are longer. A *cyme* is basically a composition of threes in which the center flower has only a peduncle, the other two being on pedicels. It is usually compounded into a many-flowered cluster. Where the two pedicels are united with the peduncle, two small basal leaves, called bracts, are attached. *Phlox drummondi* is an example.

MAKING THE FLOWER FORMS

SINGLE FLOWER.   Figure 20 shows a half-inch plastic disk pierced with two holes, covered with a thin sheet of cotton, and wired. The flower will be constructed on the top of the disk. To make this form put the ends of a two-and-a-half-inch piece of green covered wire through the holes in the cotton-covered disk, making the shorter end one inch long. Press the wire flat on the top of the disk, then bend the ends beneath it to the center and firm them with nippers. Twist the ends together *twice*. Make sure that the disk and wires are firm to avoid a wobbly head. But do not twist the wires too many times or the finish will not be smooth when they are wrapped together with the wire that forms the stem.

The size of the disk to be used is determined by the size of the shells, the amount of space required for the center, and the size of the flower it will support.

FLOWER USED WITHOUT A STEM.   Figure 21 shows a two-inch plastic disk without holes, for flowers without stems, such as water-lilies and Southern magnolias, which are to be imbedded in floral clay.

DOUBLE FLOWERS.   A two-inch plastic disk pierced with numerous holes is shown in Figure 22. Such a disk is used for wired shells when a large double or semidouble flower is being made of heavy shells that require stout stems. Each shell has two holes drilled through it and a fine wire is inserted through each one. The wires are pressed together gently with the fin-

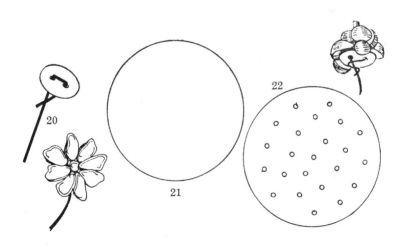

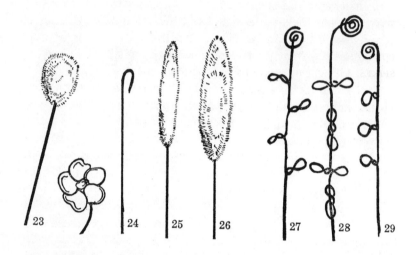

gers and their four ends are united at the base of the shell and twisted together gently. It is sometimes necessary to put two petals through one hole in the disk to make a fuller, more uniform flower. The hole at the center is reserved for the stem wire which is inserted from beneath it to slightly above it for secure anchorage.

Some shells are as hard and brittle as porcelain, and careful manipulation is necessary when they are drilled and wired. When drilling them, place the shells on a piece of cork or soft wood to reduce the hazard of breaking them.

GLOBULAR FLOWERS.   Figure 23 shows the base for a globular flower form such as a large pink or white clover blossom. A single length of wire serves as a base for the cotton and as a stem for the flower. Wrap the upper part of the stem with alternate layers of glue and cotton, making the outer layer cotton. Then mold the ball to the size of a large marble. When the cotton and glue are nearly dry, apply a final layer of glue and affix the small shells.

TINY INDIVIDUAL FLOWERS.   Figure 24 shows a #28-gauge green-covered wire with one-sixteenth of an inch or slightly more turned back over a small piece of cotton and pinched together with nippers. It is for flowers that are too small for the tiniest possible disk of coiled wire. Saturate the bit of cotton with glue and flatten it with a toothpick. Apply the tiny shells. A similar method can be used to make a tulip but the wad of cotton should then be at least a half inch thick.

SPIKES.   A spike consists of a single stem with stalkless flowers. Figure 25 shows a slender spike made by wrapping and gluing layers of green-dyed cotton around a wire to a thickness of one-eighth of an inch and a length of two to three inches from a slightly tapered top. The length of the spike depends upon the heights of the flower arrangement planned. Individual flowers, previously made, are glued directly to the cotton. If too much cotton is visible after the flowers have been glued into place, fill in the open spaces with one to three shells of the kind that were used for petals. Place them just beneath the edge of a flower so that they will appear to be partially hidden blooms.

Spikes vary in nature both in size and shape. Figure 26 shows a broad spike three-eighths to one-half inch thick and three inches long. It has been made on a single stem by alternating layers of glue and white cotton. It is advisable to work on such a spike from the top downward. Put a little glue on the upper part and arrange small shells close together on it. Then continue with glue and shells to the bottom of the spike.

Figure 27 shows a flat spike made of green covered wire with twisted loops. The distance allowed between the loops depends on the size of the shells that are to be used. Start at the top with small shells and add those of larger size as you work downward toward the base. Twist each loop twice so that the spike cannot be pulled apart easily. Glue one shell on each loop unless the spike is to be used in a round bouquet. In that case, glue shells back to back on each loop so that the spike will look finished from all angles.

Figure 28 shows a spike in which the loops are arranged closer together so that each alternate pair can be twisted toward the back. This provides more space for larger shells or small flowers so that one will not interfere with another.

ONE-SIDED RACEME.   In figure 29 all of the loops face in the same direction. This stem is for a lily-of-the-valley or a similar

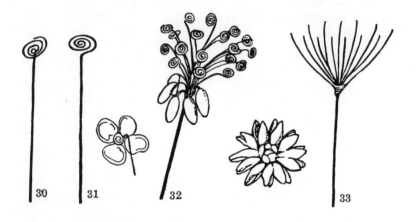

one-sided raceme. Curved downward around the edge of an old-fashioned bouquet, such sprays provide a dainty and effective finish.

SMALL SINGLE FLOWER.   Figure 30 shows a green covered wire coiled at the end for flowers too small for disks. The coil varies in size from one-sixteenth to one-quarter of an inch and is designed to support a previously made flower.

In Figure 31 the coil of wire has been turned to an upright position to support a different type of flower. The length of the wire depends upon the type of flower or flower cluster that is contemplated.

FLOWERS IN CLUSTERS.   Figure 32 shows a rounded umbel, more or less semicircular in vertical outline and consisting of many flowers. In constructing it, use half-inch disks for one-inch flowers or make quarter-inch coils for flowers that are made separately. The flowers around the edge of the cluster need longer wires than those in the center. Bring all of the peduncles to one central point, grade their length, and shear where necessary to tape them onto the stem. Then wrap them all together with Floratape.

An umbel with a flat top, shown in Figure 33, is usually composed of small flowers. Peduncles and stem are put together in the way described for a rounded umbel in the preceding paragraph.

Figure 34 shows the structure of a cluster of flowers composed of numerous smaller umbels. Queen Anne's lace is an example. Other semiglobular forms are composed of pediceled flowers on peduncles. To form the latter, allow one pedicel to be longer than the others. For example: a seashore hydrangea (hortensia) has pedicels of flowers wrapped together at intervals. Three flowers in a group are usually sufficient. The wires need to be long so that when the flowers are wrapped together the remaining pedicels can form a peduncle. The long peduncles are then attached to a stem.

A raceme, Figure 35, is a more or less loose cluster of flowers on peduncles, arranged on a stem at intervals from the top downward. The length of your shell raceme will depend upon the height desired for the bouquet. A shell-flower raceme

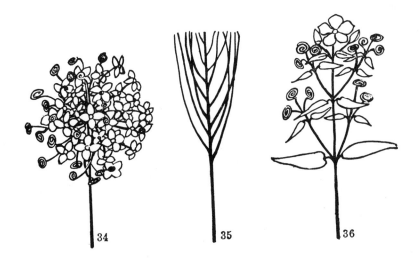

34   35   36

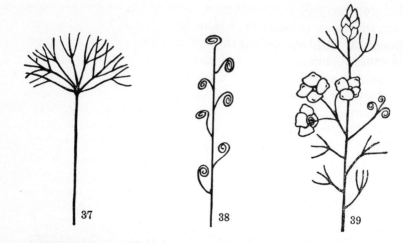

37   38   39

is more graceful in appearance if the upper part is furnished with somewhat smaller flowers. This flower form is sometimes referred to as a simple panicle. Use individually made flowers, or wired univalves, for variety.

A compound panicle, shown in Figure 36, is constructed by wrapping two or more pedicels of slightly varying length. The wires, wrapped together to form one stalk, become a peduncle. The peduncles are then attached to the stem at intervals. The length of the pedicels and peduncles is determined by the type of flower that is being made. There are loose and dense forms, and large- and small-flowered ones. Lilacs are an example of a dense form with small flowers.

Figure 37 shows a globular cluster, the Japanese snowball. To construct it, glue white flowers on wire coils. Bring all the wires to one point with the lower flowers on shorter pedicels, then wrap them together to make a stem. The flowers should form a solid ball, with no wires showing. The lower flowers are bent toward the stem.

Figure 38 shows a corymb. Notice the alternate (actually a spiral) arrangement of the peduncles on the stem; they vary in length to form a flat top.

Figure 39 shows a cyme. Notice that the flower at the top has only a peduncle, whereas the others are pediceled and arranged in threes. Where the pedicels are united with a peduncle, two small basal leaves are attached. Small elliptic slivers can be cut from a plastic leaf or green-dyed fish scale and glued to the junction. The colorful annual *Phlox drummondi* of our gardens, and its wild relatives that carpet Texas and Florida roadsides early in the spring, are examples of cymose clusters.

These then, are the basic forms used in constructing shell flowers for bouquets and other arrangements. Before going into the details of flower construction, let us, in the next chapters, make a survey of the materials that are used for various flower parts, and for buds and leaves.

PLATE 10   Bailer shell from Australia on tripod. *Courtesy* Stix Rare Shells.

6 FLOWER PARTS AND BUDS

We have surveyed the multiform shells that will simulate the petals of our flowers and discussed the basic forms that will be used to support them. Let us now consider what we shall use for buds in our arrangements, and materials that are suitable for the centers of flowers with their delicate stamens and pistils. The appearance of a shell flower can be made or marred by details such as these.

BUDS

Univalves of various sizes and colors or closely matched valves paired and glued together with a bit of cotton and a stem wire make effective buds for shell flowers. For the buds of fairly large flowers, two species of conch shell are eminently suitable. Both kinds are approximately two inches long. One (the Philippine conch) is somewhat bulbous in form and is white flushed with a yellowish tan. The other is more slender, often mottled on the outer side which has an irregularly toothed, slightly rippled, violet lip. Toward this lip run fine, dark, closely set stripes.

When these shells are used for buds an opening must be ground at the nucleus for the insertion of a stem wire. Using an electric drill, make a hole just large enough to accommodate the wire.

Pale yellow or white olive shells, ranging in length from small to about an inch and a half, are excellent for other buds. One-inch shells are good for the buds of average-sized roses and smaller ones for small roses. All univalves need to be ground down at the apex, or nucleus, for wiring. After grinding, if interior obstructions interfere with the insertion of a wire, loosen them with a point of an ice pick and shake out the pieces and other debris. Push a small piece of gluey cotton into the hole, then insert a wire that has been wrapped thinly with a bit of gluey cotton.

Deeply crinkled jingle shells make fine poppy buds. Select two valves that fit together fairly closely at the margins and glue them together with cotton and a stem wire. If the hinges at the base of the shells interfere with the snug closing of the margins, remove with sharp shears just enough of the hinges to accommodate a wire.

Small buds heading flower clusters are made of pairs of shells of the same kind that were used for making the flowers. Wrap the tip of a short length of green covered wire with the needed amount of gluey cotton and set in place two shells with their hinges closed. Use just enough cotton to hold the wire and the valves firmly together. Narrow elongated buds are made of the shells called Job's tears with the rounded parts at the top. The pointed ends are partially hidden by one or more rows of buds, followed by little flowers.

CENTERS

The stamens, pistils, and other parts of live flowers vary widely in color, size, and shape but a wealth of natural-colored small shells and parts of larger shells is available to simulate them. Perhaps the rarest color among tiny shells is yellow. It is therefore necessary to tint little lilac shells. Lightly bleached baby whelks are usually white with a pale yellow nucleus like a little knob. When more yellow is needed for certain flowers these too can be tinted and used. Yellow-dyed crushed garfish scales also are useful. To represent stamens sprinkle the crushed scales lightly in the center of the flowers where small petals meet.

To make a buttonlike center, such as that in a daisy, build up the cotton in the center and cover it solidly with crushed garfish scales.

Baby whelks are used in centers with their points either

up or down, depending upon the flower. For a low dense center snip off the points (reserving them for other uses). When the bulbous parts are placed uppermost they spread outward over the petals. If the knobs should be high—to conceal the hinges of certain shells—do not remove the points. For slender stamens, arrange the points to extend upward and outward. Lilac shells, which are very small, can be used loosely in the center of some flowers; in others they are glued rather closely together. In either case they should be arranged in a circular row with their hinges facing toward the center.

Often a single shell can be used as the center of a flower. There are many kinds from which to choose. Small- to medium-sized shoe button snails are intricately sculptured and marked with fine brown rings; when bleached they are pure white. Both versions have their uses. Small tegulas are of different colors and ornamented with circles or spots of contrasting hue. Live barnacles are tubular in shape and white with violet streaks; bleached ones are white. Small streaked ones are interesting as centers of single flowers made of lavender or violet coquinas. If the tube of a large barnacle is used, insert a slender cerith or a few dentaliums in the hollow and glue it with a piece of cotton. The shaded blue-gray coiled snail is flat and especially suitable for the center of a single or semidouble poppy.

Segments of black and blue chitons are spectacular in white flowers when arranged as a solid rosette. A circle of them filled with broken dentaliums is used for another kind of flower. The two end segments of small chitons form a circle when they are put together. This arrangement in a daisy made of ribbed mussels enhances the blue color of both species.

When a small round snail is used as a center, the flower can be embellished further by surrounding the snail with small white cup shells. For a fringed effect use small coquinas of any color that harmonizes with the petals.

For flowers as large as four inches in diameter there are brilliantly colored shells such as those of the Cuban tree snail. Equally effective are tops cut from large Philippine periwinkles. Tops from tulip shells are often washed up on Florida beaches. Some are too jagged to use; others can be leveled with a grinding wheel attached to an electric drill.

Very small orange calico scallops and jingle shells, found on Florida beaches, are often used to surround a small snail. Small jingle shells are less colorful than mature ones, but mature shells can be easily snipped to the desired size with shears. In many cases a pair of small shells of the same species used for petals makes a satisfactory center. This is especially true when flowers are made of Morton's cockles.

Colorful trap doors from univalves are also used for flower centers. Quantities of them have come into the market recently and common names have not yet been invented for them. To distinguish them their technical names must be used. The operculum of *Turbo fluctuosa* comes from the west coast of Central America. It is whorled with a combination of green, yellowish-tan, and creamy-white color. In size it ranges from one-eighth to about an inch. The very small ones are excellent for small flowers. Medium-sized ones seem to have been made to order for daisies. If they are dull you can brighten them by dipping them quickly into the muriatic acid solution described in Chapter Three (page 32).

Another interesting and colorful trap door that is useful as a flower center is from *Turbo chrysostomus,* a native of the Indo-Pacific. These trap doors vary in their coloring. Some are shaded from orange to dark brown at the rounded top and are suitable for the centers of black-eyed Susans. Others are shaded from blue to almost black at the top and are used in poppies.

The rarest operculum is from *Turbo sarmaticus,* which is native in the Cape Town region of South Africa. The trap door is usually sold with the shell. It is white or off-white with minute bubble-like projections which grow closely together. Little imagination is needed to see its resemblance to the center of a cushion daisy, or florist's chrysanthemum.

Cup-and-saucer limpets of various sizes are also useful for centers. They are most effective when the cups are exposed to view in the center of concave saucers. Some species have smooth saucers; others have larger saucers with ruffled edges. No additional shells are needed when these are used as centers. An African patella, more or less oval in shape, is more than an inch across. The inside of the cupped shell is yellow with an orange spot and fine black stripes that radiate intermittently from near the center toward the rim. Glue the concave side of a shell into the center of a large white flower. Some shells of the same species are white with black stripes and are most effective in flowers made of colored shells.

Plant materials that are used for centers include the processed buttons of live daisies and yellow mustard seeds. Cloves, peppercorns, and the dark bulbils from the seaweed called sargassum, found in warmer parts of the Atlantic, also are used. And there is another sea plant, which I have been unable to identify, which provides useful platelets surrounded by a thin ruffled fringe of the same dark color. Another useful material is cut from the woody conelike seed capsule of the casuarina tree. When used in a poppy, the flat cut side is glued down. If used in a yellow pond-lily, the cut section is glued to the base, or the whole seed capsule is used. A thin coat of lacquer should always be applied to plant materials used in shell flowers to waterproof them and make them glossy.

The whole bony skeleton of a spiny sea urchin—a model of architectural beauty—is sometimes used for a center. These animals are washed ashore on southern beaches and their shells are crushed underfoot, exposing skeletons that become bleached by the sun. Those that are naturally dried and bleached are less messy to handle. Just blow the sand off. They are likely to break if they are washed. Use the little skeletons entire in poppies and other large-cupped flowers. If they break apart, the long hooked pieces can be used as anthers in certain flowers. Whole skeletons should be lacquered to help hold the parts together.

In Chapter Eight, which tells how to make flowers of different species, definite information is given about shells suitable for the centers and petals of different flowers.

7 FOLIAGE FOR SEA SHELLS

Just as foliage enhances a florist's bouquet, dainty sprays set off the flowers made of sea shells. It is not always necessary or even advisable to use the leaves that go with the particular flower species. Like the florist, who uses sprays of hardy huckleberry and salal leaves, trimmings from yews, and various ferns in his arrangements, we can select whatever foliage seems suitable.

PLASTIC FOLIAGE

Plastic foliage is highly recommended for use with shell flowers because it is washable. Ferns and small- and large-leaved sprays of other plants can be cut apart for proper proportion. Broad leaves, often too pointed to simulate the natural shapes of those that grow with flowers, can be rounded at the apex with shears or cut to a suitable size.

For tall bouquets complete fronds of plastic maidenhair fern, or other sprays, are used. For others, these sprays can be cut into sections to conform with the height of the flowers. The secondary sprays are short-stemmed and should be cut close to the main axis. The two basal groups of a spray have angled stems. These can be imbedded in the center of a container to extend outward, or can be attached to the stem wire of a flower with Floratape. As soft and pliable as plastic leaves are, their stems are rigid. They cannot be bent to curve or droop unless a stiff coated wire is attached to the major stem.

Broad leaves of any size have to be arranged on their original stem. Philodendron leaves look better if they are pushed closer together. If the leaves are to form a rosette around an individual large flower, push their short petioles into floral clay around the edge of a receptacle that is flat or footed. Round leaves for water-lilies are not obtainable and the peltate form cannot be simulated. The best you can do is reserve the largest leaves from sprays and trim them to a roundish shape.

Sprays with leaves an inch or an inch and a half long are usually in sections which can be cut apart for use as individual sprays. Rose, geranium, and leaves of other flowers are reproduced in plastic but are usually attached to the stems of flowers. This makes buying them quite uneconomical because the flower is useless for our purpose.

FISH SCALE LEAVES

Fish scale leaves are more satisfactory than plastic for small-leaved sprays but making them involves considerable work. When arranged on wire stems, such sprays are pliable and can be arranged in any graceful position desired. Most of the kinds of scales used can be bought at shell shops.

To prepare fish scales for use as leaves wash them thoroughly, dip them in a chlorine bleach solution, then rinse them. Remove any excess water by patting them between towels. Prepare a green dip (Rit or Tintex), let it cool, then immerse the scales. (Hot dye solutions will curl scales into useless scrolls.) Thick scales will absorb the color more slowly than thin ones, so be patient. Test a few scales in the dye for color. If the color is not deep enough, reheat the water and add more dye. If the color is too deep, add cold water. When sprays of leaves have been wired, brush or spray them with lacquer to seal in the dye and make them waterproof.

TARPON fish are not sold legally. However, some fishermen will scale a fish for a friend. Special attention must be given to tarpon scales when they are cleaned and tinted. This is especially true of the large ones, which may be two or more inches across. The longer these scales are in water, the softer they become. When they are dyed and wet, use towels to absorb excess water, then place them between dry towels or blotting paper and weight them down between two boards to keep them flat until they are thoroughly dry.

To wire a "leaf" punch two small holes through the base of the scale opposite the scalloped edge, and through each hole put a four-inch length of spool wire. Bring the four wires together and twist them twice. Wrapped with green Floratape, these short wires become petioles, or stalks, that are wrapped alternately to a main stem. Large tarpon scales are good for geranium leaves. If a tall spray is needed, the lower leaves should have longer petioles than the upper, smaller ones. If the stem is to be densely foliaged, arrange the leaves closer together on a stem.

CARP scales are thicker than most of the others, oval in shape, about an inch across, and smooth around the edges. Short and medium-tall sprays made of them serve many purposes. These are prepared like tarpon scales except that they do not need to be weighted when drying to keep them flat.

After carp scales have been individually wired, attach a thin coated (or covered) flexible wire to the leaf wires. The wires of leaves below the first one should be wrapped smoothly for about an inch. Wrap from two to six leaves to the stem of the upper leaf, in pairs, for a simple spray. Compound sprays are formed by attaching the wires of three to five simple sprays to a main stem.

BONEFISH scales are small and notched at the edges. They are useful in constructing sprays of maidenhair fern. Prepare the scales in the way described for carp scales and wire them with two-and-a-half-inch lengths of fine spool wire. Use fine green for an initial stem. (This wire is more pliable than coated wire and curves more gracefully.) Wrap three to five unwrapped scales to it alternately, using narrow strips of brown Floratape. Wrap several of these simple fronds to a thin flexible coated wire to make a frond of medium size. For large fronds wrap several medium-sized fronds to a firmer stem wire. The flexible fronds can be bent into any graceful position desired.

GIANT GARFISH scales are used flat in rather shallow shadow boxes and on panels. Dye them green, as described. Groups of three to seven suggest rose leaves. Green-dyed bones of the same fish are excellent for leaf stems. They range in width from one-sixteenth to about one-eighth of an inch or slightly more. The thinnest ones are best for dainty leaf stems. Glue the stems to the background and the leaves close to them. Larger bones are used at the base of a bunch of flowers with the widest end at the bottom. The thinnest bones, dyed brown, are used for the stems of maidenhair fern. No container is used for this type of bouquet.

PARROT FISH scales are not easy to obtain but if you are fortunate enough to get some you will find them especially useful for flat picture work that is framed and glassed. These scales are naturally green or greenish-brown in color and do not need to be dyed, but should be lacquered.

PLATE 11 Imperial volute from Sulu Sea, Southern Philippines, in shell stand. *Courtesy* Stix Rare Shells.

8 MAKING THE FLOWERS

We are now ready to try our hand at constructing the flowers themselves. Before going into detail about the shells most suitable for the petals and centers of each kind, let us see how the different forms described in Chapter Five are put together.

MAKING SINGLE FLOWERS

To make a single flower an inch and a half or more across use a plastic disk prepared with wire and a thin sheet of cotton (Figure 20, page 41). Lift the cotton that has been held in place by the wire and glue it to the disk. Smooth the cotton neatly and put a little more glue on top of it. Arrange the shell petals around the edge, leaving an open space in the middle of the disk for the inclusion of a flower center. The size of this space is naturally determined by the type and size of the flower. Disks used for single flowers of various sizes should be large enough to hold the petals but not so large as to be visible between the petals or beyond them. If the open space turns out to be too large for the intended center, add another row of somewhat smaller shells of the same kind to make a semidouble flower.

Flowers that are too small for a half-inch disk can be made individually on a sheet of pliable plastic or oiled glass (page 37), with a thin cotton underlay. When the glue is completely dry, transfer the flowers to short-stalked wire coils (Figures 30 and 35). The green color of the wire coils would show through thin light-colored shells, so if you use them glue a piece of cotton between the flower and the coil. Instead of a bit of cotton a small disk of green coiled wire can be used as a base for tiny flowers.

Another satisfactory way to make single flowers is to use a ring of wired chenille cord or a pipe cleaner to hold the outer row of petals in place. For flowers that are almost flat, a pipe-cleaner ring is best because it is thinner. Chenille cord can be adjusted to support shells for flowers that are slightly or deeply cupped. Make a ring of the proper size on a sheet of glass or plastic. Put a piece of gluey cotton in the center and imbed the edges of the shell petals in it. Do not allow the cotton to reach beyond the base of the flower.

MAKING DOUBLE FLOWERS

To make a double flower, arrange the outer row of shells within the ring as described in the preceding paragraph. Put a thin layer of gluey cotton at the base of the first row of petals and add the second row of shells close to the first. Build up the center with more gluey cotton and add another row of shells. Continue in this fashion, using shells of smaller and smaller size and building up the elevation of cotton until the center is reached. When the glue is dry and the petals firmly set, remove the flower from the ring. It can be used stemless for a panel arrangement. If it is intended for a bouquet, glue a wired disk underneath it and wrap the disk wire and a stem wire together with green Floratape.

For a double flower such as a gardenia a half-inch wired disk is used and the largest and longest shells are glued around the rim. Additional rows of smaller shells are added with the very smallest in the center.

When very heavy shells are used for a large double flower they are drilled and wired to a perforated disk (page 41).

Flowers to be used in arrangement without stems are built on a layer of cotton superimposed on a solid disk (page 42).

FLOWERS IN SPIKES

Looped wires (Figures 27-29, page 42) are used for spikes of small flowers. Zebra shells—from one-eighth to three-eighths of an inch in size—with yellow lips and fine black stripes are useful and colorful for making some spikes. Glue the shells back to back on the wire loops, graduating the sizes from small at the top to large at the base. Another sort of spike, with loops not as close together, is for separate small flowers. Each alternate pair of loops is twisted to the side or near the back before the flowers are glued into place. This form of spike will accommodate flowers that are needed without their interfering with one another. A narrow spike wrapped with green cotton (Figures 24-26, page 42) can be used as a base for different kinds of individually made small flowers, constructed of such shells as small rose cups, white cups, and small Morton's cockles. A tiny shred of white cotton under each flower will prevent the green color from showing through. Once the flowers are in place, the green cotton will show very little and will suggest a stem. Should too much of the base be visible, add from one to three shells close to the flower to make it appear to be a partially hidden one. Before attaching the flowers, be sure to coat the cotton with glue to make it water repellent.

FLOWERS FOR RACEMES AND PANICLES

Single shells, univalves, are sometimes used for flowers in racemes and panicles (Figures 35 and 36, page 44), or small individual flowers may be made and applied. In making such a spray, use shells of a single species in graduated sizes. Begin at the tip with the smallest shells and wrap them to a wire stem with Floratape. Bleeding tooth shells are among the most satisfactory ones, but since these are rather heavy, a hole should be drilled through the bulging side high enough not to show from the side with the lip. Coil a wire slightly, cover it with a piece of gluey cotton, and insert it from the lip side. Press it against the shell and use more gluey cotton if necessary to bind it securely. At the same time bend the wire downward over the bulge on the opposite side. When the wires are firmly attached and the glue has hardened, wrap a stem to the first and smallest shell. Allowing one inch of wrapped wire for each peduncle, continue to wrap remaining shells alternately along the stem. The intervals of spacing are optional. The length of the raceme will depend upon the height of the bouquet you are planning.

Handsome large racemes can be made with white one-inch snails. Just above the lip of these shells there is a rounded yellow protuberance, and the rest of the shell is finely sculptured. Prepare the shells as described for the bleeding tooth panicle, above, but arrange them opposite each other, rather than alternately, on the stem.

Sprays of pendent flowers can be made of small univalves of various species, colors, and shapes. Besides the bleeding tooth shells, suitable ones are the virgin nerite, small- to medium-sized olive shells, and snails. To the back of any of these glue a coil of green-covered wire with a straight end for a short peduncle. The opening in olive shells is visible and their length makes them appear more pendent than round shells. All the other shells mentioned should be wired so that the lips are at the bottom.

Another raceme of one-inch white snails is of special interest. Just above the lip of these shells there is a rounded yellow protuberance, and the rest of the shell is finely sculptured. Prepare the shells as described for the bleeding tooth panicle, and arrange them opposite each other, rather than alternately, on the stem.

MAKING DIFFERENT FLOWER SPECIES

Similar techniques and the same or similar shells are used for making the various flowers that are members of the Rose family. These include the blossoms of apple, cherry, peach, and plum trees, of hawthorns, strawberries, and quinces, in addition to the garden roses and the wild kinds. The same is true for members of the daisy or Composite family—flowers that are formed of many minute flowers (called *florets*) in a compact head. Among these are the white or ox-eye daisy of the fields, the brown-eyed Susans, sneezeweeds, Jerusalem artichokes, sunflowers, chrysanthemums, asters, and others. How to make these and many other kinds is told in the pages that follow. Flowers are listed alphabetically by their common names. Their botanical names, as well as the scientific names of the shells and other items used, are given in the index.

It should be noted that many species within a genus produce different forms of flowers and flower clusters. This gives a wider scope to the imagination when beachcombing for shells or purchasing them for flower making.

ANEMONE (See Japanese Anemone)

APPLE (See Fruit Flowers)

ARTICHOKE, JERUSALEM (See Daisy and Daisylike Flowers)

BLACK-EYED SUSAN (Brown-Eyed Susan, see Daisy)

BRIDAL-WREATH. Bridal-wreath sprays are composed of very small white umbels among small leaves. They are short-stemmed and grow intermittently along slender arching branches. Make the tiny five-petaled flowers individually, using the smallest of white cups. Glue a tiny yellow mustard seed in the center of each one. Transfer the flowers to tiny coils of wire on one-and-a-half-inch "stems." Wrap a group of flowers together to form an umbel about one and three-eighths of an inch in diameter. When a number of umbels have been made, wrap them rather closely to a flexible stem wire. Between them wrap small fish-scale leaves, or leaves cut from plastic foliage sprays.

BROWN-EYED SUSAN (See Daisy)

BUTTERCUP. A buttercup can be made of five bright yellow cupped jingle shells. Construct it on a piece of glass, pliable plastic, or its equivalent. For a center use very short pieces of dentaliums or the snipped long ends of baby whelks, which suggest stamens.

For a semidouble globe-flower, which is related to the buttercup, use a half-inch disk and glue jingle shells slightly below it. The inner rows are started near the edge of the rim. The flower is globular in shape and up to one and a half inches across. To attain the globular shape use gluey cotton under the shells to mold them to the disk.

The florist's ranunculus, another relative, is fully double and very handsome. The flowers come in white and in several shades of yellow and orange. For petals use large cupped and rounded jingle shells. To construct a flower about two inches across use a one- or one-and-a-quarter-inch disk. If smaller shells are used in the center, the base must be built up with gluey cotton. Since this flower is also globose, the shells are glued around and around each other in a spiral. Pare the hinges of the shells for proper shaping of the flower.

BUTTERFLY-BUSH.   The butterfly-bush, or summer-lilac, produces a slender, densely flowered panicle of small blossoms resembling true lilacs in color. It can be best reproduced as a raceme. Make small four-petaled flowers separately, using tiny white cups or pink rose cups, and glue a small, pale yellow mustard seed in the center of each. When the glue has set, transfer each flower to a wire coil overlaid with a thin piece of cotton. The "stems" of the coil wires should vary in length from one to one and a half inches. Wrap small buds, made by gluing together two small shells over a piece of cotton and a wire, for the top. Add a few more buds below the first group to start the shaping of the panicle, then start to wrap a stem to the buds. Next wrap short-stemmed flowers into the main stem. Continue to wrap flowers with increasingly longer peduncles until the desired width is attained, then taper the panicle toward the base. The flowers should be arranged so closely that the wires are barely visible.

CALLA LILY.   A large fig shell is eminently adapted to conversion into a calla lily. Although the colorful part of the flower is white or yellow, we can be content with the beige color of the shell because of its form. Nature provided the shell for the flower; all we need do is add a stem. Glue a coil of green wire on the rounded end and wrap it to a stem wire.

CANTERBURY BELLS.   Because Canterbury bells are sometimes four feet tall, the flower spikes or sprays are made smaller than natural size when they are reproduced in shells. Use janthina shells for the five-lobed, bell-shaped flowers. Three species of lavender and purple-shaded ones float ashore on the east coast of the Florida Keys.

For the spike or spray use a long piece of thin green-covered wire. Make alternate loops in the wire, spaced to accommodate shells of increasingly larger size, with the smallest loops at the top (Figure 27, page 42). Apply a wisp of gluey cotton to the top loop and set the smallest flower in place. It should project outward and upward. Proceed downward until all of the flowers have been glued to the loops.

Janthina shells are extremely fragile and should be handled with special care. If their lips become chipped, soak the shells in water for an hour and then smooth them by cutting away the rough edges a little at a time with manicure scissors. Shells that are slightly chipped, forming a toothed lip, are not objectionable.

Because they are so delicate, shell sprays of Canterbury bells are best displayed in a glassed picture frame of shallow depth. They are not suitable for bouquets.

CARNATION AND PINK.   Carnations and garden pinks are made of kitten's paws. Select shells that have fine- or coarsely-toothed edges. Some of these shells are pure white, others are colored on the outside and have dark hairlines at the edges that accentuate the dentate margins. The inner white side of the shells should be visible. For a large carnation use a three-quarter-inch wired plastic disk, and begin by gluing shells around the rim. Then, holding the disk in the palm of your hand, slightly cup the outer row of shells to shape the flower. Continue to fill in the flower, using narrower shells as you approach the center. Short shells can be elevated by adding more glue and cotton. Such flowers can also be made in a chenille ring and mounted on a wired plastic disk if they require stems.

The garden carnation is smaller than those grown by a nurseryman. A reasonable imitation of a rather small carnation can be made by using fewer kitten's paws with deeply serrated margins. For semidouble flowers use pale yellow bleached or natural-colored baby whelks or broken dentaliums in the center with their points upward to suggest slender stamens.

CHINA ASTER.   China asters are large double flowers up to two-and-one-half inches across. They may be white or come in shades of blue, purple, or pink. To copy them in shells, use purple, pink, or white coquinas of medium size.

Roll a wad of cotton in the palms of your hands to make

a ball five-eighths to three-quarters of an inch in diameter. Anchor it with a little glue to oiled glass, then add the shell "petals," or rays. Make sure that the hinges of the shells all face in the same direction.

Begin the flower at the base. Put a little glue on the long point of the broad end of the first shell and push it under the cotton ball. Add the next shell, making sure that it overlaps slightly the hinge of the first one. Continue adding shells in this way until the row is finished. The second and third rows are added in the same way, except that the tips of the shells are pushed into the cotton ball.

After completing the first three rows, flatten the top of the ball slightly and glue a circle of very small shells in the center with their points overlapping. These will suggest unopened florets. Around this circle add slightly larger shells, gluing them so that they stand upright with the pointed end out to the height of the unopened rays. Add two or three more rows, using shells a little larger for each row, until the cotton ball is covered.

CHRISTMAS ROSE.   Christmas roses have five broad petals and conspicuous stamens. Use glossy white or light-colored rounded shells for petals. The center of each flower has three parts. In the middle glue a small round top of a baby whelk or a sargassum bulblet. Surround this with a row of pale yellow lilac shells, then surround the circle of lilac shells with a row of very small ceriths with their broad ends spreading outward. These flowers are less than two inches across and have long stems.

CHRYSANTHEMUM (See Daisy)

CLEMATIS.   Flowers of clematis vines are white, deep purple, violet, pink, and rose. A shell imitation should not exceed two inches if it is to be used in a mixed bouquet. Larger flowers are effective in more pretentious arrangements. Use six or seven opalescent Maine fresh water mussels, white tellins, Bahama rose petals, tulip mussels, or hooked mussels on a wired disk of suitable size. For stamens use broken tooth shells, a single large barnacle that is not too high, or a circle of blue chiton plates. If large chiton valves are used for large flowers, smaller ones can be glued inside of them, or the open space can be filled with dentaliums. It is often important to provide contrasting colors of petals and centers. This is especially true when the flowers are large.

CLOVER.   Pink clover blossoms are made of small rose cups on a globose base of cotton (Figure 23, page 42). Select shells of similar size and some that are smaller so as to fit better near the stem. If you spread the shells on a flat surface, it will be easier to pick them up with tweezers and apply them to the glue on the cotton ball. For this type of flower the glue is spread at first only on the upper half of the ball. Start at the top by gluing in an inverted shell. Then continue with rows of shells until the upper half of the ball is covered. Now spread glue on the lower part of the ball for more rows of shells, and continue until the entire ball has been covered. It is best to apply the glue a little at a time because it dries quickly. Be sure to set the shells close to each other. For a clover that is not fully open, and for deeper color, glue the shells with the budging side out and the hinges up. For lighter pink and more open blossoms, glue the bulging side of the shell to the cotton with the hinges at the base.

CRAB-APPLE (See Fruit Flowers)

CROCUS.   The crocus is a cupped flower an inch or more long on a four- to six-inch stem. Reproductions can be made with white, yellow, lavender, or purple coquinas for petals, glued with their hinges at the base of the flowers. Use as a base a wad of gluey cotton pinched together at the end of a stem wire, or a half-inch wired disk. The cotton base is more satisfactory for a flower that is almost closed; the wired disk is better for an open cup-shaped flower. The bulged portion of the shells should be on the outside to help form the cupped shape. In the center of the cup glue three yellow baby whelks with their points up. A chenille ring can also be used to make the flower and hold it in shape until it is dry. Under the finished flower glue a tightly coiled green wire for a base. To the straight end of the wire wrap a stem wire.

DAHLIA.   Only the small varieties of dahlia are suitable for reproduction in shells, and these may be double, semidouble, or single and of any color except blue. Most of the colors needed are available in coquinas. Use a one- or one-and-a-quarter-inch wired disk for a flower about two inches across. Ample glue and cotton are needed on the disk except near the rim for the outer row of petals that are almost flat. Extend the outer petals from the disk with their hinges imbedded. Allow this row to dry completely before continuing, then add more cotton and glue to the disk. Mold the shape in the palm of your hand until the shells are set, then prop it up on a small glass (such as a whiskey glass) that will hold the petals level until they are dry. Continue with gluey cotton and rows of shells until the center is reached. In the center glue two small shells, facing each other. Shells sometimes slip out of place so watch them while they are drying and push those that become loose back into place with a toothpick. These flowers can also be made in a pipe cleaner ring and stemmed later.

For the rays of single dahlias use the largest and broadest coquinas you have on a two-thirds-inch disk for an average-sized flower. Imbed the shell hinges in gluey cotton around the disk, leaving an open space in the center for a rounded cluster of baby whelks. Use the knobby ends of the small shells at the top to conceal as much as possible of the hinges. Average-sized white tellins or rose petals may also be used for the rays. They are broader than coquinas, so overlap the hinges. For variations in dahlias, many suggestions given for other daisylike flowers, below, can be adapted.

DAISY AND DAISYLIKE FLOWERS.   Daisies and daisylike flowers are very numerous. They belong to the *Compositae,* one of the world's largest plant families, and they are often spoken of as "composites." Their flowers have a buttonlike center (except those that are fully double) and from six to many rays, or petal-like flowers, that vary in number, length and width according to the species.

The white, or ox-eye, daisy that grows wild in our fields has numerous slender rays and a yellow buttonlike center. To reproduce it, glue large rice shells around the edge of a five-eighths-of-an-inch wired plastic disk, leaving an open space at the center for the button. In affixing the shells, expose their open lips to view because these resemble the rolled rays of the flowers. For a center use a processed natural daisy button, a small trap door, yellow-dyed lilac shells with their hinges up and facing the center, or yellow crushed gar scales. Trap doors of *Turbo fluctuosa* range in size from one-eighth to three-quarters of an inch; they are round and suitably colored for the center, or disk, of a daisylike flower. If a shell makes too large a disk, add a row or two of very small coquinas to fill the space between the rays and the center, which is usually yellow.

Most daisylike flowers have broad rays that taper to a

point, though some are rounded or blunt. Coquinas provide a multitude of suitable colors for such flowers. Some are striped with black, pink, or salmon-pink at the squared top of the shells. For variety, these can be used with their stripes at the outer edge of the flower.

The Shasta daisies seen in gardens are larger than those of the field, and they are often at least partly double. Use a broader disk and coquina shells to make them. Glue the largest shells around the rim and use progressively shorter shells for the rows that follow until only enough open space is left for a yellow buttonlike center.

Cushion daisies—the alpine sorts that are sometimes grown by rock gardeners—have a larger center than other kinds. A trap door from a *Turbo sarmaticus* with its tiny bubblelike surface is ideal. If it is not available, use pale yellow lilac shells or the knobby tops of baby whelks from which the points have been removed. The rays can be made of small coquinas.

Brown-eyed Susans are larger than white field daisies, and the rays are broader. To make them use yellow coquinas with the pointed end at the outer edge of the flower on a five-eighths-of-an-inch disk. The center, which is brown, is higher than in a white daisy. Any of the following can be used to finish the flower: a rotund trap door of orange and brown from *Turbo chrysostomus*, a top slice from a casuarina seed capsule, lilac shells dyed brown, or brown-dyed mustard seeds.

Jerusalem artichokes have flowers similar in color to brown-eyed Susans. They are small dainty American sunflowers which got their inappropriate name through corruption of the Italian *girasole*, meaning "turning to the sun." Jerusalem artichokes grow wild along roadsides and railroad banks. To make them in shells, use the largest and brightest yellow coquinas on a five-eighths or three-quarter-inch disk. For a center use any of the materials mentioned for finishing brown-eyed Susans. If the hinges of large coquinas are too high to accommodate a flower disk, file them down to make them fit.

Helenium, or sneezeweed, another member of the Composite family, is a coppery red or shaded yellow. Both colors occur in coquinas. The flowers are an inch or an inch-and-a-half across with a slightly elevated yellow disk.

Red, deep coppery red, and old-rose coquinas are not as

abundant as those of most of the other colors and they cannot be bought. If you want them you will have to gather them yourself on Florida beaches, or delegate others to do so.

Salmon-pink Transvaal or Barbeton daisies are made of Tampa tellins with the glossy outer side of the shells visible. The rounded edges should be at the perimeter of a flower made on a half-inch wired disk. Fill the center with a buttonlike arrangement of yellow lilac shells or the knobby tops of baby whelks.

African daisies with blue-edged white rays are made of small Atlantic ribbed mussels. Shells may range from five-eighths of an inch to a little more than one inch in length. Glue the larger shells close to the center of a disk. The blunt end should be at the outer edge of the flower. To brighten a flower with additional blue use two end sections of a chiton to form a disk in the center of the flower. If the next smaller sections are used, bring three of them together as closely as possible by overlapping them to form a circle. In this case, have the light blue teeth at the top. Any remaining space can be filled in with small pieces broken from a valve plate of similar size.

French marguerites, or Paris daisies, have white or pale yellow rays and a center of deep yellow. This species is somewhat smaller than our native white ones. Use a half-inch disk and ring it with small pale yellow coquinas for pointed rays. Extend the small shells as far out from the center of the disk as possible and provide a center of a deeper yellow.

There is a florist's chrysanthemum, called the "anemone" type, which has many small adventitious rays around its large disk. Use large white coquinas for the outer row and small ones for the inner rows. For the center use one of the materials suggested for the cushion daisy, but make it larger. A one- or one-and-a-quarter-inch wired disk is needed to make the flower.

Small composite flowers of various sorts can be made from small mussels, lucinas, scallops, and coquinas. Use six valves of the one-inch Florida mussel with purplish streaks to make individual flowers which can be wired later. Half-inch cross-hatched lucinas can be used for another form. The bulging side of the shells should be on the outer surface of the flower which is made on a half-inch disk. Small scallop species indigenous to the Bahamas are yellow, beige, or blotched with russet. Build it on a half-inch disk with the colored side of the shells exposed. Any small yellow shells, or crushed gar scales, can be used for centers. These flowers are so small that several can be used on a single stem.

In fact, any daisies an inch or less in diameter are more effective if grouped together in a cluster. The disk wires need to be longer if several flowers are to be attached to a single stem. Combining the flowers in this way avoids an awkward clutter of stems in a bouquet.

Flowers made of Italian coquinas add interest to a bouquet. These shells are larger than Florida species, the smallest being about an inch long, and are white with large purplish blotches. Use a five-eighths-of-an-inch wired disk and provide a center similar to those described for other single composite flowers.

There are still other daisylike flowers which can add glamour to a shell bouquet. You have only to observe them in florist shops, conservatories and gardens for your creative fingers to start itching for new shells and original techniques.

For other members of the composite family, see China Aster, Dahlia, and Thistle.

DELPHINIUM.   Delphiniums bloom in long racemes with small flowers at the tip and increasingly larger ones on longer peduncles as the base is approached. Most often the flowers are blue.

Make individual flowers, using light blue chiton valves, four for each flower. Some species of chiton have a small round depression in each valve. When glued across each other, the depressions fit together and form the four-petaled flower.

Construct the flowers on a plastic sheet or on oiled glass. When they are dry, attach each one to a coil of fine green-covered wire (Figures 30, 31, page 43) with a short straight length allowed for the peduncle. The peduncles should be of graduated lengths so that the raceme will taper from small at the top to broader at the base.

When all the flowers needed have been made, bind them to a stiff wire stem with Floratape, beginning at the top with the smallest flowers on the shortest peduncles. The length of the raceme is determined by the size of the arrangement planned.

DOGWOOD.　　Dogwood flowers are the simplest of all to make. Four shells of the elegant dosinia or Florida lucina are used for the white bracts. Glue them to the outer edge of a half- to three-quarters-inch wired plastic disk with their hinges forming the tips of the bracts. Unbleached commercial shells, or shells gathered on the beaches that have retained at least part of the brown ligaments at the hinges, give the most lifelike effect.

Since dogwood flowers appear before the leaves and arise from brown branches, wrap their short stems with strips of brown Floratape. Pliable thick-gauge hardware wire can be used for flexible branches that are intended for wall sprays. For bouquets make the stems of covered or coated wire and wrap them together with the wires of the disk. Large shells can be brought close together in the center to make a flower appear smaller than it otherwise would. Cover the center with a circular arrangement of any small yellow shells or tiny zebra shells.

Pink dogwood is made of the largest rose cups, which are sometimes sold as apple blossoms. Large flowers cannot be made of these shells, for they are seldom longer than three-quarters of an inch. However, flowers one and five-eighths inches across can be made by allowing three-eighths of an inch for the center, which can be filled in with pale yellow baby whelks, the largest lilac shells, or small zebra shells. The points of baby whelks should be imbedded in gluey cotton. Lilac shells should be glued closely together with hinges at the top.

Pacific dogwood, a relative of our eastern flowering dogwood, has flowers with six petal-like bracts, rather pointed at the apex. The most suitable shells available for making these flowers are white tellins or pink rose petals.

EGYPTIAN STAR CLUSTER.　　Egyptian star clusters are rarely more than three inches in breadth. Each flower has five pointed petals and measures about an inch and a quarter across. Usually the flowers are white with an inconspicuous center. Small coquinas seem to be the most suitable shell for making these flowers. For a center use a rounded end of a natural or bleached baby whelk. Make the flowers individually and glue them on wire coils three to four inches long, then attach a stem to a group of flowers to form a cluster.

FORGET-ME-NOTS. The only blue shell suitable for making forget-me-nots is the chiton with its small light blue valves. Cut from each thin valve its rounded projections and of these make a five-petaled flower. For the yellow eye use a top cut from a very small baby whelk. These tiny flowers are best made on oiled glass with a wisp of cotton beneath each one. For a cluster to be used in a bouquet glue each of the flowers to a tiny coil of green wire and wrap them on a main stem. If the flowers are intended for a panel or a board under glass, no wires are necessary.

FRUIT FLOWERS (See also Orange). Pale pink peach blossoms and the white blossoms of apple and pear trees grown for fruit are single. For making shell flowers representing them use medium to large rose cups, white cups, or small thin Florida lucinas. In the center use either yellow-dyed lilac shells or baby whelks for stamens. Make the flowers on half-inch plastic disks or construct them individually and glue them on wired disks or wire coils.

Strawberry blossoms have white petals that are smaller than those of the peach, pear, and apple. Very small white jingle shells or medium large glossy cup shells can be used for petals. Make the flowers individually and glue them on wire coils. Centers can be glued in the flowers either as they are made or after they have been glued on disks.

Crab-apple blossoms vary from pink to rose-red. All of the shades will be available if you purchase large rose cups in quantity. The flowers grow in small clusters close to a brown stem or branch and are somewhat smaller than those of other fruit trees, so smaller shells must be used. Glue each flower on a short-stemmed green wire coil.

Quince blossoms are mostly of an orangey-red (sometimes pink or white). These and other fruit flowers can be made of shells similar to the ones we have mentioned here.

GARDENIA. Gardenias average about an inch and a half in diameter and shell imitations of them are made of Pennsylvania lucinas. Use a one-inch wired disk and glue the first row of shells around the rim with the concave side on top and the hinges imbedded in gluey cotton. Add three or four more rows of smaller shells within the outer row with their convex sides toward the center and their hinges on top. In the center of the flower glue two smaller shells with their convex sides facing each other.

A double flower resembling an open gardenia can be made of white slipper shells, which are oval or elongated, thin, and somewhat irregularly curled. Use a half-inch wired disk and glue the largest and longest shells around the rim. Continue with more rows to the middle and finish the flower with the smallest shells brought close together in the center. Shells that curve in different directions add interest to the flower. Attach a stem wire close to the underside of the plastic disk and wrap all the wires together.

GERANIUM.   Garden geraniums have umbels of one-inch flowers with a birdlike beak in the center. The size of a cluster depends upon the variety and the degree of maturity. When a cluster is fully mature all of the flowers are open; one approaching maturity has a number of pendent buds. Some flowers have rounded petals, others pointed. To simulate a cluster use medium to large rose cups, sometimes called apple blossom shells, of pale pink to rose-pink; white cups, or pale salmon-pink Tampa tellins. Make the flowers individually, using five shells for each. When the glue is thoroughly dry furnish each flower with a peduncle of coiled wire, bearing in mind that for a globular head some of the peduncles should be at least three inches long for flowers that are farthest from the stem.

In the center of each flower glue a baby whelk with the point upward. For drooping buds use a pair of one-half- to five-eighths-inch coquinas of matching or deeper color. Arrange the buds around the outside of the cluster and wrap them together at one point for almost an inch with Floratape. Trim the unwrapped portion of the peduncles to varying lengths to taper them. Wrap a stem wire twice and insert it among the peduncles and wrap them all together; continue to wrap the stem wire for the rest of its length, then bend the buds downward as they appear in natural flowers.

Rosebud geraniums grow in small umbels about two inches across. Small double flowers representing them are made individually of rose cups and white cups. Use five small shells for the outer row of petals and within this row glue about three more. Complete the flower with a center made of a closed pair of shells of the same kind. When the flowers are dry transfer them to wire coils overlaid with a thin piece of gluey cotton. Wrap the peduncles together with a stem wire as described in the preceding paragraph.

GLOBE-FLOWER (See Buttercup)

GRAPE HYACINTH.   The familiar grape hyacinth of spring is a deep purplish blue but cultivated kinds include a white form. White pikaki shells glued close together on a thick white cotton-wrapped wire will produce an interesting replica. When the basic form of glue and cotton is dry and has been shaped, apply glue a little at a time and affix the shells. Continue to add glue and shells until the spike is complete.

HYDRANGEA.   The hortensia (*Hydrangea macrophylla*), commonly grown at the seashore, produces in summer a large globose cyme of flowers with four (rarely five) white, pink, rose, or blue petals. The hortensia is also cultivated by florists for earlier flowering. Except along the coast, it is not hardy in the northern states. For replicas of these flowers select the largest rose cups or white cups and construct the flowers individually. The largest white nut clams (with their hinges in the center) are suitable for somewhat smaller flowers. To simulate the small group of tiny stamens in the center use the slender ends snipped from pale yellow baby whelks. Glue the flowers to coiled wires of various lengths. Long wires are necessary for flowers at a distance from the center of an inflorescence. Make small groups of flowers by wrapping stem wires of different lengths together with the flower heads fairly level. Start with one flower in the center of the cyme and wrap it to a stem wire. Then wrap each cluster to the stem at uneven intervals to form a dense rounded head.

Flat-topped hydrangea cymes have very small flowers with large ones interspersed near, and at, the perimeter of a cluster. The tiny flowers are made of shells called Job's tears on tiny pieces of cotton held by the bent end of a thin wire (Figure 24, page 42). The shells fit closely together and no center is needed. The larger flowers are made individually and transferred to wire coils. Centers are similar to those of the globular hydrangea. To make a cyme start with a few very small flowers by wrapping a stem to them. The peduncles of succeeding clusters must be increasingly longer to provide flatness. At the same time, successive ones should be brought close to preceding ones to avoid a conical formation.

The flower clusters of the Peegee hydrangea (the hardier shrub, with flowers that change from white to deep rose) differ from the others in shape, being pyramidal. Make the flowers as described for the larger ones of the flat-topped hydrangea. The shape of the inflorescence is controlled by the length of the peduncles that are attached to a stem. This cluster is large and densely flowered.

IRIS.   Reasonable facsimiles of irises are made of calico scallops of any matching colors. A large form is made of two-inch white bay scallops. Whatever the size, make the lower drooping portion of the flower in a chenille ring or on oiled glass or a plastic sheet. The ring method is perhaps easier because it holds the shells in place. Put gluey cotton on top of the hinges of the inverted shells and when the shells are set glue in a wrapped wire disk. When completely dry remove the partially made flower and turn it right side up. On top of the drooping petals glue somewhat smaller ones with their hinges down. Although iris flowers have three segments of each kind, six shells are usually required for the drooping petals and five for those that stand upright.

In the center of the large flower glue a Cuban snail, a fairly large top cut from a reddish tulip shell, or the top of a Philippine periwinkle. For small irises use calico scallops of smaller size and for the center use a top cut from a blue-striped western olive. Calico scallops are of many sizes and colors and all are suitable for making iris flowers.

JAPANESE ANEMONE.   Japanese anemones are reproduced in white or lavender-pink. The flowers measure about an inch and a half across and are composed of five petals with short stamens in the center. Use one-half- to three-quarter-inch wired disks. For white flowers use white tellins with their pointed ends at the center of the flower, and for pinkish ones use lavender Venus shells in the same way. A thin layer of gluey cotton on the disk will bind the shells firmly to it. If the shells are not broad enough to conceal the disk, use an extra shell. A small top cut from a Philippine beaded periwinkle or a small shoe button snail of natural color can be used to suggest stamens.

JERUSALEM ARTICHOKE (See Daisy)

LARKSPUR.   The annual delphinium called larkspur is seen in white and in numerous tones of blue, violet, and pink, and the flowers grow around the stem in raceme form. Each flower has five petals and a spur. Shell larkspurs are made of five-eighths-inch coquinas in any appropriate color on half-inch wire disks. The hinges of the shells should overlap in the middle of the disk. Sometimes, to avoid cluttering and to bring the flowers closer together, only four petals are used. In the center of each flower glue a mustard seed. When the flowers are closely arranged on a stem the omission of a shell here and there is not noticed. This is true also of live flowers unless they are pulled apart for examination, and the spurs of only a few immature flowers at the top of a raceme are visible. Spurs therefore are not attempted. Make the sprays of varying lengths and different colors for a group arrangement.

LILAC.   Flowers are clustered densely in more or less pyramidal compound panicles. Each tiny flower has four petals at the top of a narrow nectar tube. The tube cannot be simulated easily and is ignored when the flowers are reproduced with shells. For petals with rounded margins use small white cups; for curled margins use pink rose cups; and for pointed margins use glossy little white nut clams. Make the flowers individually and glue an inconspicuous, pale yellow mustard seed in the center of each one. Then glue each flower on a coiled wire overlaid with a thin piece of cotton. The end of the wire coil becomes a pedicel. Now wrap two or three of them together about three quarters of an inch below the flowers. The part that is wrapped becomes the peduncle, which in turn is wrapped to the stem.

Start the cluster with five to seven small buds at the top—Job's tears in pairs with their points down, or pairs of shells similar to those of which the flowers are made—and below them attach a stem. Surround this stem with short flower clusters, and as you proceed increase the width of the panicle gradually by adding clusters with longer peduncles. Spray lacquer on the underside of all coils and cotton-covered wires that are not wrapped with Floratape. As the cluster is formed, add a flower or two in any open spaces. At the base use flower clusters with shorter wires for roundness. Most lilac panicles are so densely flowered that their stalks are not visible.

LILY-OF-THE-VALLEY.   These are made of pikaki shells glued on loops of wire (Figure 29, page 42). Since these shells are opaque, cotton is not needed under them. The lips of the shells should be exposed and faced downward. Wires with loops on one side are used for flat arrangements. When a bunch of flowers is planned, stem wires with loops on both sides are sometimes used, but a better method is to make a single stem wire appear to support two racemes of flowers by gluing the shells back to back. The wire stems are less slender than the living ones, and if too many are used the bunch will look stiff and unnatural. The back to back arrangement shows more flowers and less wire.

Barnacles somewhat larger than pikaki shells can also be used for lilies-of-the-valley. However, they should not be glued back to back because they project farther from the loops and can be broken easily.

MAGNOLIA.   Southern magnolia (*Magnolia grandiflora*) is a large spectacular white flower framed in a rosette of large green leaves. It can be duplicated by using for petals large chalky-white macoma clam shells measuring about one-and-seven-eighths by three inches. Those that are suitable are fragile and light in weight. Select a two-inch plain plastic disk and cover it with several alternate layers of glue and cotton. Imbed six shells around the rim with their hinges at the side and running in the same direction. The abruptly bent ends of the shells should be visible. Within this circle glue another row of five shells. In the center glue a large cup-shaped African patella. The inside of the patella is yellow with an orange blotch and around it are intermittent black radial stripes that suggest stamens. No other ornamentation is needed.

This flower looks best on a flat dish or a dish with a short pedestal. Place in the dish a piece of floral clay large enough to hold the short stems of large plastic leaves and secure it. In the center imbed the disk holding the flower.

Star magnolias are smaller with a single row of six or seven slender pointed petals. Use white tellins on a three-quarter-inch wired disk. Overlap the hinges slightly so that the shells will appear more slender. Fill in the center of the flower with pale yellow lilac shells arranged with their hinges outward.

Smaller star magnolias can be made of the largest white

coquina shells on five-eighths-inch wired disks. The stem of each flower is short and attached rather close to a branch of the shrub. Imbed the hinges of the shells at the center of the disk, allowing space in the center of the flower for stamens made of baby whelks with their points in the glue. Baby whelks are long enough to conceal the coquina hinges. If the hinges are too high, they can be reduced by careful shearing. When coquinas, rather than tellins, are used for star magnolias, a few more shells are needed. Flowers about two inches across are normal for this species.

When *Magnolia soulangeana* has passed its full-blown phase its petals begin to flatten. For large flowers in this stage use a wired disk one-and-a-quarter to one-and-a-half inches across. Use large ribbed Atlantic mussels for the petals and a leveled, beaded periwinkle for a center. This magnolia flower appears before the leaves and has a short grayish-blue stem that juts out from the branch. Use flexible hardware wire wrapped with brown Floratape for a stem when these flowers are used in composing a wall spray. They are effective with dogwood and branches of other shrubs.

MOCK-ORANGE. Blossoms of the mock-orange average about an inch across and have four rounded, slightly cupped, satiny white petals and short, slender, yellow stamens. The flowers are short-stemmed and arranged in groups of three or four on slender arching branches. Make the flowers individually of white jingle shells or small white Florida lucinas from which the gloss has not been removed by excessive bleaching. For stamens use the pointed ends snipped from baby whelks. A short wire coil makes the best stem.

MULLEIN. Morton's cockles are suitable for making mullein spikes. The shells range in size from one-quarter to three-quarters of an inch and are embellished with small or large amounts of brown. The weedy mullein of roadsides has yellow flowers, but the occasionally cultivated species, known as moth mullein, is sometimes white. Although the five petals are rounded at the margins, to enhance the color in shell-flower representation, place the hinges of the shells at the margins of the flowers.

It is sometimes impossible to use five shells on a half-inch plastic disk. Try making a flower of four or five shells individually, then select a base of the proper size—either a wired plastic disk or a coil of green wire. For the common mullein, glue them directly on a cotton-wrapped wire base to make a spike of stemless flowers. Two small valves of the same shells, glued face to face, form the center of these flowers. For moth mullein, arrange the flowers on short pedicels in a loose raceme.

ORANGE.   Orange blossoms are short stalked and closely attached to the branches. They are best for very low arrangements, for panels, and for shallow shadow boxes. Make the flowers separately on glass or a plastic sheet, using either white coquinas or glossy white nut clams for petals. Use five or six shells for a flower, arranging them with their points outward, and bring them close together at the center for a finished size of one inch or slightly more. The centers of orange blossoms are small and inconspicuous. For these use small white lilac shells or very short pieces of dentaliums. Buds are made of white marginellas. Glue a green-covered wire and insert it through the canal and up along the lip of the shell. Bunch a few buds together to show the bulging sides and use them in small clusters apart from the flower.

PANSY.   Pansies are usually tricolored and have five petals. The two upper petals are of the same color, somewhat elongated, and rounded at the top. They overlap slightly. The three lower petals are of a contrasting color, somewhat smaller than the upper ones, and their arrangement suggests a superimposed three-petaled flower. In the center of each flower there is a conspicuous dark spot.

A number of shell species are suitable for making pansies, including cockles, scallops, and limpets. Morton's cockles vary in color from white to light yellow and brown. Pacific Coast tellins from the state of Washington are pale yellow, rosy orange, and white. Some have purple blotches. Small colorful scallops from the Bahamas and South Africa are also useful. In these shells the color is on the outside, so they are best for reflexed petals. Some species of limpet have characteristic dark spots; others have dark hairline margins, or dark stripes that radiate from the dark spot. They seem to have been designed for the centers of pansies.

Construct the flower on oiled glass or on a pliable plastic sheet. Put down a little glue and press onto it a thin piece of white cotton. Spread more glue on the cotton, then gently press into place the two upper shells. Just below these, and over-lapping them, glue two more shells with their hinges at the center. Next glue the bottom shell down broadside with its hinge also at the center. In the small open space, glue the rounded side of a limpet so that its rim extends over the hinges of the three lower petals.

If a stem is desired, make a coil of green-covered wire with the stem part five inches long (Figure 30, page 43) and glue the coiled disk to the center of the pansy behind the petals.

PEACH (See Fruit Flowers)

PEAR (See Fruit Flowers)

PEONY.   Use a one-and-a-half-inch plastic disk with numerous holes (Figure 22, page 41). Pure white, thin, curled oyster shells make the best petals, and they are plentiful on the sandy beaches in the vicinity of San Diego and Coronado, California. These shells range up to two inches in size and look contorted. They are so thin that two holes can be easily pierced through one of the narrow ends for wiring. Press the wires together very carefully, for the shells are fragile. Bring the wires together at the base of the shell and insert them, with the wires of other petals, through one of the holes in the disk, reserving the center hole for the stem wire. Arrange the shells closely on the disk, then draw all the wires to the center underneath it. Insert the stem so that it extends just above the disk and wrap all the wires together. Between the wired shells glue smaller ones that have been prepared with gluey cotton at the base. Any spool wire that is visible between the shells can be concealed by using gluey cotton over the base of one shell and adjusting another to it by pressing them together.

POND-LILY.   Two-inch (or larger) buttercup lucinas are used for making yellow pond-lilies. These shells are white with circular yellow to orange bands. Use a two-inch plain disk (Figure 21, page 41) covered with glue and cotton so that the hinges can be deeply and firmly imbedded. Arrange four shells around the rim of the disk, then glue four more close to them inside. The nearest approach to a satisfactory center is the conelike fruit of the casuarina, or Australian pine. These trees abound in the southern half of Florida, and the woody capsules can be gathered from the ground beneath them. Imbed a single flow-

er in floral clay on a flat dish with one large round plastic leaf.
POPPY.   Semidouble poppies are colorful and they are easy
to copy. Irregularly shaped large white, yellow, orange, or apricot jingle shells are best for their petals. Arrange the largest
shells around the edge of a five-eighths-inch wired disk. Glue
a row or two of smaller jingles inside the row of large ones. A
natural-colored bluish coiled snail makes a good center.

A handsome single poppy is made of five or six white or
bright yellow Japanese scallops that have a crinkled appearance. Some shells have an indefinite blotch near the center. For
two-inch shells or smaller ones use a half-inch wired disk and
glue the hinges around the rim to form a cup. For centers use
a blue-black trap door, the whole skeleton of a spiny sea
urchin, or a top cut from a casuarina seed vessel with the flat
side uppermost.

PUSSY WILLOW.   For the "pussies" of pussy willow sprays,
use the common bubble shells. Wrap a short length of thin wire
with a wisp of cotton and coat it with glue. Insert the wire
through the opening in the shell. When you have prepared as
many "pussies" as you think you will need, and the glue has
dried thoroughly, wrap them to a "branch" of sturdy wire, using
brown Floratape. Start with a shell at the very top and wrap
others close to the stem spirally, until the stalk is the length
you want.

QUINCE (See Fruit Flowers)

ROSE.   The Rose family includes hundreds of species with
flowers of many colors and shades. Apple, cherry, and peach
trees and strawberry plants are members of this large group
(See Fruit Flowers). Single flowers of the Rose family have five
petals. During their life cycle these flowers change from a
cupped shape to a flat-petaled one. In double forms the outer
petals sometimes become reflexed.

Semidouble and double roses of various colors and characters can be made of large pink rose cups, large white cups,
and white, yellow, apricot, orange, and shaded jingle shells.
These roses vary in nature from miniature to two and a half or
more inches. Their petal margins may be rounded or curled.
Some are loose-petaled, others have petals that are closely and
symmetrically arranged. The form of a rose can be varied by
using shells in different ways.

Miniature roses are best made individually and glued to

a base of green coiled wire (Figures 30, 31, page 43). To prevent the green color of the wire from showing through the shells, overlay the coil with glue and add a thin piece of white cotton. Add more glue and then set the flower in place. The glue binds the flower solidly to its base and, incidentally, waterproofs the wire coil.

A single miniature rose requires five petals of small pink rose cups or white cups. The center of each flower can be finished with a small loose cluster of yellow lilac shells, points of young whelks facing upward and outward to suggest slender stamens, or a yellow mustard seed. A semidouble rose needs only three additional shells, set inside the row of five petals, and mustard seed or pair of lilac shells cupped together for a center. Miniature flowers are more colorful if the shells are placed with their hinges outward and upward. These little roses are excellent for arranging in spike or raceme form.

For a sweetheart rose use a half-inch disk to allow for a final row of larger shells that are glued just below the disk. Cotton should be used at the edge of the disk to round the double flower at the base. With a toothpick push glue-saturated cotton into bulges wherever it is needed so that a contact is formed between the shells and the disk.

An open rose is made of the largest rose cups with their hinges at the outer edge to simulate curled petals. For a two-inch flower use a three-quarter-inch wired disk and extend the shell hinges as far from the disk as possible to get the maximum-sized flower. Glue the rounded ends of the shells flat to the cotton. Continue toward the center with rows of shells and increase the height of the flower gradually by adding cotton and pointing the shells slightly upward until the disk is almost completely filled with shells. In the center glue a pair of smaller shells together to complete the flower. Wrap a stem wire twice with narrow strips of Floratape, bring the stem close to the base of the disk, and wrap all the wires together. Continue wrapping to the end of the stem.

Tea roses are closely petaled and can be made of large rose cups or jingles on three-quarter-inch disks. A one-inch disk can be used for larger roses made of jingle shells. Use the largest shells at the rim of the disk so that no part of it will be visible when the flower is finished. If smaller shells are used for the inner rows add extra gluey cotton to raise them to the proper level. Some beginners find it easier to start a double rose from an elevated cotton center and to apply shells of increasing size for succeeding rows.

Jingle shells are useful for making somewhat larger roses. The tones of the shells vary considerably, making them suitable for different kinds. Those especially desirable are clear in color and include white, pale and lemon-yellow, apricot-orange, orange, and shaded. Their shapes also vary and they range in size from a half inch to an inch and a half or more. Sort the shells for color, then select those that are suitable for roses.

When a rose has passed its prime, the outer petals recurve. This phase can be duplicated by inverting jingle shells and gluing them to the base of the almost upright shells that form the outer row. The hinges of the inverted shells should face toward the stem. A tiny shred of cotton and glue between the shells will bind them together securely.

To adjust cupped jingle shells with strong hinges that interfere with the proper shaping of a flower, cut a small wedge out of the hinge with sharp scissors or wire shears. Cut carefully, removing a small amount at a time, then trim away any bits that prevent the shells from fitting properly. Cutting beyond the hinge weakens the shell and induces peeling. The outer rounded margin should not be trimmed, no matter how irregular its shape may be, to preserve the natural thin edge of the shell. Not all flowers are perfect and some irregularity often lends interest.

Shrub roses are loosely petaled and shells used for them need not be as perfectly rounded as for certain other roses. Smaller and somewhat closer fitting jingle shells are used in the center of a disk to start a flower. A gardener may visualize a rose with a looser center. Either way is satisfactory as both kinds occur in nature. Irregularly shaped shells for shrub roses give the flowers a casual, shaggy, more interesting appearance.

The Chinese shrub rose with its small single yellow flower can be simulated by using half-inch yellow jingle shells. The flowers are very short stemmed and grow along the terminal branches.

SHOOTING STAR.   For making shooting stars use Tampa tellins. Glue the shells upside down on a piece of gluey cotton placed on oiled glass or a plastic sheet. Arrange the shells with their points toward the center. The form should be cup-shaped.

When the glue is dry remove the form from the glass, turn the cup upside down, and on top of it glue fewer shells to form a narrower cup. When dry, insert under the inverted cup a small wired disk padded with gluey cotton. The depth of the inverted cup makes it impossible to wrap a stem wire with those of the disk, therefore this should be done before the disk is inserted.

SNOWBALL (Figure 37, page 46)

STAR-OF-BETHLEHEM.   Flowers have six slender white petals and they grow in groups of twelve or more. Make one-inch flowers individually and mount them on wire coils. Use white coquinas for the petals. A small yellow or brown mustard seed or a bulbil from sargassum weed can be used for a center. Wrap a stem twice and insert it among the peduncles to the point where they all meet and wrap all of them together down to the end of the stem.

An exotic relative of the star-of-Bethlehem is *Ornithogalum arabicum* with white flowers of the same size but with broader petals. Each flower has a conspicuous black pistil. For petals use white cups or the small glossy white nut clams found on the west coast of Florida. The tips of the petals are sometimes abruptly pointed, sometimes oval. The flower peduncles are attached to a stem to form a close rounded head. Make each flower individually and in the center glue a large ball from sargassum weed or a black peppercorn. If neither is available, use the ball part of a clove.

STAR-FLOWER.   These grow individually and are of lavender and violet shades rather than white like the star-of-Bethlehem. Otherwise they are very similar. Use six small coquinas for each flower and construct the flowers individually, then glue each one on a four-inch wire coil and attach a wire stem. For stamens sprinkle some crushed gar scales in the center. Although each of these flowers has its own stem, it is more convenient in a shell flower bouquet to group a few together with long peduncles and attach them to one stem.

SUN-ROSE.   One of the sun-roses has five rounded and cupped yellow petals with a large purple eye and grows to about one and a half inches across. Use bright yellow jingle shells on a five-eighths- or three-quarter-inch wired disk. The flower disk is higher than in the ox-eye daisy, and a good effect is obtained by using purple-dyed baby whelks with their points stuck into the glue. For a rounded shape select the longest ones for the middle and grade to shorter ones around the circumference of the circle. A blue-shaded trap door of *Turbo chrysostomus* is good for the center.

THISTLE.   Plumeless thistles, with their odd purple flowers, are sometimes planted for bold effects in gardens. To reproduce them for a shell bouquet you will need the purple white-knobbed spines of a kind of sea urchin that inhabits Puget Sound. Select spines that are from three-quarters to one inch long.

For a full rounded flower, roll cotton in your palms to make a ball about half an inch in diameter. Taper it a little at the base, add a dab of glue, and place it on oiled glass. Start building the flower at the top. Apply glue to the thin end of the spines and push them into the cotton. When you reach the outer circumference of the flower, start using shorter spines but keep the form slightly rounded. Green-dyed cotton at the base of the flower can represent the calyx. Lacquer the cotton to smooth it and to keep the dye from running.

TORCH-LILY.   The torch-lily, or tritoma—also called the red-hot-poker plant—can be simulated only in form. Use coquina shells on a base of stem wire wrapped thickly with cotton and tapered toward the top. Glue the backs of the valves to the cotton with their points up and about three inches from the top of the raceme draw the flowers closer to the stem. Orange and yellow coquinas and shaded shells of these two colors are best.

TULIP.   The species and cultivars (hybrids) differ in the form of their petals but all have six—three inner and three outer ones. The petals are of uniform length, whether pointed or rounded. Suitable shells for slender tulips such as *Tulipa clusiana* include shaded pink sanguins, purple-shaded tulip mussels with the outer skin removed, large Florida rose petals, or the larger Bahama rose-petals. More globose flowers can be simulated with white, yellow, or mottled egg cockles. The simplest and most satisfactory way to make a tulip is to use a built-up chenille ring to hold the shells upright. Test it for correct size by placing the shells in the ring temporarily and adjusting it.

When the ring has been adjusted, put the necessary amount of glue and cotton on a pane of glass or a plastic sheet within the ring. When the three outer leaves have been glued in, add three more close to them inside. The juncture of the inner shells should be in the center of each outer shell. Before the glue is completely dry, pierce a hole through the center of the cotton for a stem which will be inserted from beneath when the flower is dry.

The color of a tulip petal at its base inside the flower sometimes is different from that of the rest of the petal. Chiton sections can be arranged in a circle inside to simulate this variation if the opening is large enough or, if you can find them, you can use tops cut from blue olives or small Philippine tectarius shells. Within the circle glue a slender cerith or a very few broken dentaliums to form the center.

VIBURNUM CARLESI shrubs have two-inch umbels of small, pale pink flowers. On thin bits of cotton make very small four-petaled flowers by gluing white cups or pink rose cups on a sheet of plastic. When they are dry transfer each flower to a wire coil with a straight end two and a half inches long. A group of about fifteen flowers is needed. Bring all the wires to a single point and graduate them, then wrap them with a stem. A small yellow mustard seed can be glued in the center of each flower while it is being made on the sheet, or after it is wired.

ZINNIA.   Doubles are made of coquinas of various colors with the broad end at the outer edge of the flowers. For a mixed bouquet the flowers need be no more than two inches across. Use a one-inch wired disk, or make the flower in a pipe cleaner ring and add a stem when it is dry. The outer row of shells is almost flat and succeeding rows are elevated gradually with gluey cotton to form a shallow dome. Semidouble zinnias are flatter and require a yellow center. Use baby whelks with their points up.

Many other flower species can be made of shells; to describe them all would be impossible. As you gain skill with practice, you will find yourself instinctively selecting the proper shells and centers for the flowers you wish to make. And now, before ending this chapter, a repeated warning: be sure to apply lacquer or glue to all parts of flowers that are not already waterproof. Waterproofing preserves seeds and causarina cones and prevents the rusting of wires; it enables you to wash your shell flowers without fear of damaging them.

9 ARRANGING THE BOUQUET

When you have made enough flowers to plan a bouquet and have prepared sprays of suitable foliage, your next step is to select a container that is suitable in size, shape, and color for the composition you have in mind. A plain or footed vase or urn, a large sea shell, or an attractive piece of driftwood can be used.

In order to focus interest on the flowers, the container should be neutral in color. White, leaf-green, and delicate pastel shades are good. Green harmonizes nicely with the flowers and the other colors merge into the background, leaving the flowers dominant in the composition. Decorated containers are not desirable because they distract the eye.

Alabaster urns, either pure white or white mottled with gray, are often an excellent selection. They have solid bases with short pedestals and flaring mug-shaped tops. An urn about eight inches tall and six inches wide at the rim of the mug is good for long-stemmed flowers, some of which should be two or more inches in diameter for a mixed bouquet. The flower stems at the center of the arrangement should be erect, and the outer sprays should curve gracefully outward to conform with the flaring rim.

An urn or vase of this same size is also useful for arching branches of flowers made of large and smaller shells of the same species. For good proportion, the sprays at their highest point should measure one and a half times the height of the container. They can be extended outward to any width desired. A few large individual flowers at the bottom center of such an arrangement give the impression of weight. The upper parts of the sprays should be furnished with smaller flowers for airy grace.

Another footed container of suitable shape resembles a small bird bath. This type is especially good for a rounded bouquet of short-stemmed flowers designed for a table. For a large dining table a larger container of the same shape can be used, but include in your composition a few flowers with longer stems. Maidenhair fern leaves, drooping slightly over the rim, provide an effective finish.

A narrow vase is suitable for arrangements that follow the Hogarth line, which is a loose letter S. Bind or bend the flower stems together, using large flowers in the center of the S and smaller ones toward the ends. Short sprays of plastic fern leaves should be bound to the flower stems to keep them from springing back to a stiff position.

SHELLS AS CONTAINERS

Large shells often make very attractive containers. When the outer skin has been removed from them they are rarely highly colored. But avoid shells that are conspicuously marked unless the bouquet is to contain some flowers of similarly colored shells or with conspicuous centers that pick up the colors of the blotch or streak.

Oval shells are good for arrangements that are to be placed against a wall, or when flowers are needed only three-quarters of the way round the shell and are backed by foliage. The most pleasing composition is one that conforms to the outline of the shell. The flowers can be of different heights and those at the side should extend outward. A few larger flowers, tucked deep into the bouquet near the center, add interest to such arrangements. Several small-flowered sprays can surround the shorter-stemmed large ones.

All shells used as containers need to be provided with feet to prevent them from rocking. Glue from two to four small snail shells at strategic places under them so that they will be held solidly level. If a large shell is used, such as a whelk or horse conch, use the snail known as shark eye or other large species. These can be applied to make the shell lie flat or to keep it slightly lifted at the narrow end. Either position is satisfactory. However, if the narrow end of a horse conch is raised higher than the bulging portion, sprays of small flowers can be extended along the opening of the canal. The outline will be something like a reversed cornucopia. The largest flowers are anchored in the bulbous part of the container.

Sometimes coral heads, cut level across the bottom, are used flat-side down to support a flower-laden shell. Or the leveled bottom can be anchored to a flat container with the spires pointing upward. In this case, the tallest spires are treated as flowers and small dainty flowers and short pieces of fern leaves are glued in the hollows. Since the background is white, the flower stems are wrapped with strips of white Floratape. Test the flowers in the crevices before you glue them permanently.

FOR SHADOW BOXES

Shadow box combinations require careful planning because the size of the bouquet and its container is severely limited by the size of the frame and the depth of the box. For a box with an inside measurement of twelve by sixteen inches, a vase no more than four or five inches wide and three inches high is needed. It is difficult to find containers for shallow boxes, but they can be improvised from pieces cut from a tin can and painted, or molded by a ceramist and cut in half lengthwise before being baked in the kiln. The outline of such compositions is usually made with flat ferns, their stems imbedded in floral clay and their tips one half to one inch from the frame. The bouquet is built up with flowers, beginning near the top center of the container with those that are largest and most deeply colored.

If the box has a depth of one and a half inches the flower arrangement must be no deeper than one and a quarter inches. However, some of the flowers can be two inches across and arranged intermittently at and near the center of the bouquet.

Other flowers, about an inch in depth and width, will give the composition a three-dimensional effect which can be accentuated by small-flowered sprays of summer-lilacs, used at the outer circumference. Rather flat sprays in between, intermingled with sprays of small fish scale leaves, extend about an inch from some parts of the sea-green backboard. The container is held in place with floral clay.

PACKING THE CONTAINER

When you have selected a container, pack it to a suitable depth with hard green floral clay into which the stems of the shell flowers will be pushed. If the container is light in weight, pack it quite solidly so that the flower arrangement will not be top-heavy. Sometimes, when not too many stems are involved in a bouquet, a layer of Styrofoam is used between the clay at the bottom of the container and the covering clay. If only a few light sprays are used, a block of green Styrofoam alone will serve to anchor the flowers. Fasten it in the container with special adhesive tape available at florists' shops.

BASES

Bases of driftwood do not require floral clay if they are used for wall arrangements of flower sprays. A very effective composition consisted of a branch that suggested a leaping lizard. From its neck swished long sprays of white, orange, and purple flowers. The wall of the living room against which it was displayed was of antiqued cypress, and to accentuate the arrangement black molding was used to simulate a frame thirty by thirty-six inches.

Slender manzanita branches can serve as a base for a table decoration. Tiny twigs that interfere with the flowers are cut off and all flower stems are wrapped with brown Floratape which is less conspicuous than green when twisted around the branches. A few large flowers are wired in the center of the spray to give it width. On either side, along the branches, are somewhat smaller flowers. The ends of the branches are tapered by the smallest flowers and buds.

10 CARING FOR YOUR
SHELL BOUQUET

Loving care and hours of painstaking craftsmanship have gone into the construction of your shell bouquet. Take care of it properly and it will last for years.

Do not place it in bright sunlight or the colors of the flowers will soon fade. Even the most beautifully colored shells that are washed up onto beaches fade when they lie in the sun for several days.

If your bouquet is not being used, protect it from dust. Cover it, container and all, with a thin transparent plastic bag of the type dry cleaners use for clothing.

We have stressed again and again that all dyed materials used in making shell-flower bouquets should be brushed or sprayed with lacquer to make them waterproof. Seeds and parts of plants that are used in centers should also be lacquered to prevent them from disintegrating. If your bouquet has been made waterproof you can wash it.

WASHING

A demonstration of washing usually makes spectators gasp as if they expected to see the bouquet fall apart. However, the floral clays we have recommended will hold the flowers firmly in place.

Make a solution of mild soapsuds. Invert the container with its flowers, holding it so that the fingers extend over the rim. Swish the bouquet gently back and forth in the soapsuds, then rinse it with fresh water. Shake off the excess water carefully and turn the container right side up. Any moisture that remains will soon evaporate. Should any white spots appear on flowers that have been washed (assuming that the shells were clear when the flowers were made), roll a small piece of cotton on the tip of a toothpick, dip it in baby oil, and coat the spotted shells.

DUSTING

Small bouquets can be freed of dust by simply holding them under gently running water. If care is taken to prevent a heavy accumulation of dust, bouquets should not need washing more than once a year.

REMOVING FLOWERS

If for any reason a flower is to be removed from its bed of floral clay, grasp it by the stem with your fingers or with pointed nippers. Pulling it out by the head is likely to separate it from the stem. If a flower head has been pushed askew, put two fingers under it to bend it gently into place. Careless handling may not only damage the shells of a slanted flower but break the petals of an adjoining one.

PACKING FOR SHIPMENT

Before packing a shell bouquet, put tissue paper between all of the flowers that nearly touch each other to avoid the breaking of delicate petals. Next cover the whole arrangement with a loose plastic bag and tie the bag to the vase well below the flowers.

If the bouquet is round, it should be tied upright in the center of a sturdy carton. Select a strong carton and reinforce it, if this seems desirable, with corrugated board or sections cut from another box. Place your shell bouquet in the center of the carton and mark it for two holes to be pierced in the bottom on each side, parallel to the narrowest part of the vase. Remove the bouquet and punch the holes. Pull stout cord or cloth tape through the holes to the inside of the carton, allowing enough length to tie two ends from each side around the vase to hold it securely in place. Pack crumpled newspaper, tissue, or excelsior into all open spaces around the container. Put two or three sheets of tissue paper on top of the bouquet, and seal the carton. Wrap it in heavy Kraft paper and mark the package "breakable" and "glass." A careful shipper in Palm Beach, Florida, uses popcorn to fill open spaces around tissue-wrapped fragile shell ornaments.

Flat bouquets are prepared for packing in much the same way. They need only one piece of cloth tape, run through holes pierced in the bottom of the carton, to secure their containers. Lay the prepared bouquet on tissue paper, tie it down firmly, and fill in all open spaces at the sides of the vase or urn with crumpled paper. Cover the bouquet loosely with tissue paper. Seal with tape, wrap, and mark "breakable, glass." (Sometimes it is a good idea to strengthen the bottom of the carton with another piece of paperboard.)

Wrap individually stemmed flowers separately in tissue paper. Make a bed of crumpled tissue paper in the bottom of the carton and arrange the first layer of flowers on it. Continue layer after layer with crumpled paper over each one. Cover the last layer with more crumpled paper, then seal the carton, wrap it in Kraft paper, and mark the carton "fragile."

Shallow or deep shadow boxes can be shipped safely in a sturdy carton of appropriate size. Antique shadow boxes have been delivered intact, wrapped in an old soft piece of cloth to protect the glass and the fine old finish on the frames. Wrap paper over the cloth and secure it with masking tape. Put plenty of crumpled newspaper in the bottom of the carton and place the shadow box on top of it. Fill in all sides of it with more crumpled paper and add a layer to the top. Seal the carton, wrap it, and mark it "glass" and "breakable."

11 SHELL MOSAICS

Mosaic art is of ancient origin, but shells were not used in making designs until late in the eighteenth century. Shell ornamentation is seen on altars and in niches of some European churches of this period, and in England the ceilings and walls of homes were sometimes decorated with shells and naturally colored stones. An occasional chair was often embellished with shells set in the legs, arms and back, and English literature tells of a duchess and her daughter who spent several years on such a project. Outdoors, shells were sometimes used to border flower-beds or to hide cement work.

In France, wooden and ceramic vases were covered completely with shell mosaics. Shells used for some of these, seen in private collections, were set in glue. Most of the vases held shell flowers and were protected with glass cases decorated with ormolu. Poorly preserved relics of this period can sometimes be picked up in European antique shops and market stalls. They have even found their way to second-hand shops on lower Third Avenue in New York City. Cleaned down to the base, one of these was found to be a well-turned vase of pear wood. Most of the flowers it contained were faded and all were soiled, but some were restored to their original beauty.

A modern version of mosaic decoration, stunning in its effect, can be seen in the Fish House Restaurant in Naples,

Florida. The ceiling beams and pillars are encrusted with shells from every part of the world. They are set in grout (a cement mixture) and are every conceivable size and shape.

MOSAICS FOR BEGINNERS

In hobby shops where instruction is given in shell mosaic work, a decorated glass or ceramic vase is usually the beginner's first project. Shells of various sizes are provided and a box of commercial plaster.

If the vase is of glass, the first step is to coat it with lacquer. The plaster is mixed according to the directions on the carton, and is applied to no more than one-third of the surface at a time. Its thickness depends upon the size of the vase. A base that is too thick will distort the shape of a small vase. If the vase has a neck, you start decoration there. The plaster coating on the neck should be thin and the shells should be small and flat. Add plaster to no more than one-third of the surface at a time and place the shells carefully.

OUTDOOR PROJECTS

A PATIO WALL.   A more ambitious undertaking, after some skill has been attained, might be a section of a patio wall—perhaps behind a fountain or low-lying pool.

For this type of work there are two kinds of grout, each permanent and each of special value. The first calls for two parts of cement, three parts of fine white sand, and one part of slaked lime. For the second, use one-third lime and two-thirds cement, by weight. This is an all-white mixture that makes some shells look lighter in color than normal. If desired, the grout can be tinted. About seven colors are usually available in department and hobby stores. Always blend your ingredients carefully before adding water.

Another mortar mixture recommended consists of two parts fine white sand, two parts plasterer's lime, one part light cement. Mix thoroughly, then add enough water to make a soft putty-like mix that will hold its shape. One standard sack of sand, one of lime, and one-half sack of cement is sufficient to cover about 35 square feet. But only enough for immediate use should be mixed at a time. Lime in a grout mixture makes the cement harden faster. When it is omitted more time can be allowed for arranging the shells or correcting a design. Sand gives the mixture a rougher texture. A grout mixture is recommended for mosaics with visible openings between the shells. If the shells are to be fitted together closely, pure cement is used. Only a small amount is prepared at a time. To prepare any of the mixtures mentioned, add water slowly and stir until the mixture has the consistency of paste.

Cover only a small area at a time and, after placing the shells, wipe them clean with a short-handled squeegee. Then run a sharp-pointed stick along the narrow crevices between the shells to smooth the finish. Open spaces between the shells can be filled with nacreous cuts or broken bits of shell to add lustre to the design. Some experts recommend keeping the finished work covered with a damp cloth for several days so that the grout will not dry out too rapidly.

Since a section of wall behind a fountain or pool is less exposed to damage than a wall in an open location, the shells can be arranged to project outward in a three-dimensional effect. The pattern can be informal or random. Do not, however, use shells that are fragile.

King's crown shells (*Melogena corona*) can be set in the form of a crown. Also effective in such a location are two species of scorpion-shell with short curved legs and unusual shading. One species has shading that goes from orange to white. The other shades from white to purple and has fine, close, almost black stripes running from inside the center of the lip halfway to the edge. These shells should be pressed into the grout with the rounded side down. Another species that can be used is a soft luminous white shell flushed with gold (*Bathybembix argenteonitens*) from the Asiatic coast and nearby Japan. It measures about two inches across and is shaped like the dome of a mosque. The large tiger-cowrie (*Cypraea*) is colorful, glossy, and suited to some designs and cones (*Conus* species) are also useful. These vary widely in color and marking. There are other suitable shells too numerous to mention.

A SEASCAPE on a cinder-block wall of a patio of a beach house created by William Justema, a mosaic artist, is unusual and effective. Broken and fragmented shells, clusters of barnacles, water-washed stones, glass marbles and other beach drift, along with small glass tesserae encrust the panel, which has a plywood base and a wooden frame. In the center is a swirl of slender, curved shell pieces that represent a large loose-petaled flower. In two effective places near the frame are individual five-petaled flowers made of small shells. Glass marbles and tesserae add color and luster to the composition.

PATIO TABLE.   Patio tables with mosaic tops can be of wood or wrought iron. They can be made especially for this purpose or adapted to it. Unfinished tables, designed for the addition of a tile top, are suitable. Or a wooden table can be prepared easily for this use by nailing a molding five-eighths of an inch high around the four sides.

If you make your own table, use three-quarter inch plywood for the top. Around it nail a molding one to one and a half inches high. This should come just below the plywood and rise about half an inch above it. If the shell top is to be depressed below the top of the molding, the strip may be higher. The thickness of the shells will largely determine the size.

Seal the plywood and the inner side of the molding with Laticrete Bond or a similar waterproofing material. Before the sealer dries, sprinkle on coarse sand or bird-cage gravel. This will strengthen the bond between mortar and wood.

A mortar bed for a table should be about three-eighths inch thick. Smooth it with a mason's trowel. For greater evenness, use a home-made gauge—a flat piece of wood which is laid on the molding and worked around the edges and corners of the still soft table top. Let the mortar set for two to two and a half hours. Then press fairly flat shells, such as the flat valves of scallop shells, into the mortar, and fit them together as closely as possible. To level depressed areas, fill in with groups of very small shells or shell fragments. For more brilliance, press in small bits of broken glass or irregular glass tesserae. Edges that are beveled on the upper side scintillate more brilliantly than straight-cut ones.

Work carefully, remembering that the design must be level and flush with the rim of the table. You can be sure that it is perfectly level if you press a board down gently on the shells. Continue filling in small areas and, as the work progresses, place small shells between the larger ones to cover the top completely.

To surround a motif, or to make a border at the edge of the table, marginellas (*Prunum* species) of uniform size are suggested. These are tropical shells—polished, oval, and more or less spiral—with a few rough teeth on the edge.

SHADOW BOXES

Dainty mosaics of shells and shell flowers are made for display in shadow boxes. Fragile shells can be used for them because the boxes are hung on the wall like pictures, safe from harm.

To make a shadow box, you construct sides for a selected picture frame to give it more than normal depth. The box may be deep or shallow, open or covered with glass. If covered with glass, a backboard is usually screwed to the frame, the glass being permanently attached to the front. The backboard and the inner sides of the frame are painted sea-green, pale blue, or bluish-gray or lined with wallpaper or art paper of these colors. If the frame is oblong, it can be hung either for width or breadth. When hung for breadth, it can be used for a broad bouquet arranged in a low container. Suggestions for bouquet arrangements are give in Chapter Nine.

For a mosaic of shells and shell flowers you should have a rather large collection of very small colorful shells and some of larger size. When you have a sufficient number, make a plan of symmetrical design suitable for the frame you have selected. The depth of the shadow box will depend upon the depth of the shells and shell flowers that will be used. Patterns may be simple or intricately detailed.

Such arrangements are modern versions of an almost forgotten Victorian art. Not all of the old ones included flowers and none has been seen with foliage. Some of the frames used had removable backs. In others the glass was removable. Such mosaics are not to be confused with "sailors' valentines," believed to have been made in Barbados, that usually included Cupid's darts, hearts, and sentimental phrases spelled in shells.

Some consisted of two small, hinged frames that folded together and were fastened with a hook.

Some of the valentines and a few of the old mosaics have survived and can be seen in museums and private collections. Among them is a flower mosaic in a round sixteen-inch frame that was made in France. The background is painted light green and on it is a crescent of shell flowers. The frame is glassed.

MAKING THE MOSAIC DESIGN

It is easy to draw a mosaic design if you take it step by step. First make a model by drawing on paper heavy enough to hold its shape that has been cut to fit the backboard of the chosen frame. Measure the cut paper from top to bottom and from side to side and mark the exact center with a dot. Then proceed to draw as follows:

1. Draw the outer circle, using a pencil tied to a string of the proper length that is fastened at the central dot with a thumb tack. The circle to be drawn should be about one-quarter of an inch from the edge of the paper. Holding the pencil carefully erect, draw the circle. (The other circles can be made in this same way or by using a compass, dish, cup, or glass.)

2. Decide how wide you want the circular band of flowers to be, adjust the string on the pencil, and draw the second circle.

3. Using a compass or a dish, draw the third small circle. If you use an opaque dish and cannot see the central dot, measure the distance from the edge of the dish to the second circle and indicate by pencil dots where the new circle should be drawn.

4. With a ruler, divide the inner circle into six or eight sections by drawing lines through the central dot to opposite sides of the circumference.

5. Hold a ruler or yardstick across the paper and draw a line from one corner to the first circle, and continue it from the opposite side of the circle to the other corner. Draw a similiar line from the other corner to the opposite corner.

6. Between each two corner lines, at the outer circle, draw two semi-ovals. Triangles will be formed automatically. If flowers are not to be used between the second and third circles, draw with a ruler four wide-open Ws to form narrow and wide triangles.

7. Cut a piece of wallpaper or art paper, preferably green, the size and shape of the paper on which you have drawn your design. Set this aside temporarily. Place tracing paper on the model paper and trace the design on it. Then put a sheet of carbon paper, carbon side down, on the green paper and the tracing paper with the design on top of the carbon paper. Hold these three pieces of paper firmly together so that they will not slip and go over the design with a tracing wheel to transfer it to the green paper. Brush wallpaper paste on the back of the green paper and smooth the paper onto the backboard. When it adheres tightly and the paste is completely dry, begin to fill in the sections with shells.

FILLING IN THE DESIGN

The smallest shells are used in the center. Glue one round shell in the middle of the circle. If the space is very small, use a cup-shaped shell such as a roundish patella or a cup-and-saucer shell. Use shells of different colors in each small section, alternating light and dark colors for contrast. In the outer band fill the triangles with reasonably small shells; in the lower part of semi-ovals fill with somewhat larger shells; and set the largest ones in the outer parts of the ovals near the frame. When all of the sections have been filled in, arrange previously made shell flowers in the open band and in the corners of the square shadow box.

A twenty-two-inch square mosaic and flower box was made recently (page 100). Although most Victorian designs were octagonal in shape, this one is nevertheless a modern interpretation, more colorful and detailed. In the center is a circle divided into eight triangles. Two rings, one of tegulas and another of catfish pearls, outline the circle.

The second circle has sixteen divisions. In the smaller triangles are glued shells slightly larger than those in the mid-

Figure A
a. Largest shells for mosaics
b. Intermediate size shells
c. Band for flowers
d. Two circles of shells
e. Smallest shells

dle sections, and in each wide open W are glued shells that are larger still. Both sides of the open band are outlined with green limpets and within it is a wreath of shell flowers of many kinds and colors. Some of the flowers project almost two inches from the back board and almost touch the glass. Other flowers are raised on bases of gluey cotton. Small flowers in groups have short stems to allow them to be twisted into desired positions. Short sprays of tiny flowers were made as if for bouquets. Their stems were wrapped with thin pieces of cotton and then glued into the band. The ends of the stems were concealed by gluing a flower close to them. Small flowers, or fish scale leaves, were glued into the open spaces, or a short spray of very small flowers was tucked under the elevated flower.

The circular motif left four corners of the square open. These were also filled with flowers, buds, and leaves. Large flowers were used in the largest spaces and the design was tapered with slender sprays where the circle came close to the frame, making the spaces narrow.

Three kinds of colorful and interesting trap doors are featured in this arrangement. A Central American species is in the center of a daisy in the upper right hand corner, an orange-brown one from the Indo-Pacific is in a brown-eyed Susan on

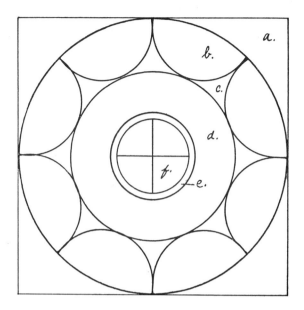

Figure B
a, b. Largest shells for mosaics
   c. Intermediate size shells
   d. Band for flowers
   e. Two circles of shells
   f. Smallest shells

the right hand side under the wreath, and a South African species is in a cushion daisy in the lower left hand corner.

An eighteen-inch octagonal mosaic and flower shadow box is simpler in design. The glass was glued into the grooves of the frame, and the line of junction was covered with narrow braid. White glue was used for both operations. This is a type of glue that is useful to the hobbyist in many ways because it dries clear. It is used in making lamp shades and in upholstering. Hobby shops and hardware stores both stock it.

More than 12,000 shells of about ninety-five species were used in the mosaic shown on the jacket. Parts of shells used include the ears of angel wings for a white chrysanthemum, and three species of Turbo trap doors in the centers of flowers. Pearls from catfish skeletons were used for bleeding heart flowers and a circle around the central mosaic. A whole purple urchin from Hawaii represents a cultivated China aster. Small reddish-brown spines of a Pacific stone urchin were used to compose a chrysanthemum. Pieces of plastic maidenhair fern are tucked between the flowers.

Instead of adapting a glassed picture frame for use as a shadow box, it would be better to have one made. Have the glass fixed permanently at the front, but have the backboard made removable for easier decoration.

12 UNDERWATER PICTURES

Fabulous gardens grow in warm oceanic waters, their white to brilliantly colored flora and fauna undulating in the lazy tides and currents. Perhaps you have seen them through a glass-bottomed boat or bucket during a vacation. If so, you may have noticed that several species grow habitually together in picturesque patterns. Some of the scenes are roughly rounded, luring the eye to other arrangements. Underwater pictures seek to capture scenes from these gardens of the sea.

Sea plants, commonly called seaweeds, are the flora of the oceans. Though most of them are algae, they vary widely in color, size, and form. Sea fans and sea feathers are coral formations —calcareous constructions built by tiny marine animals for their support and habitation. Like sponges, they are fauna. Some seaweeds and sponges are highly colored when they are freshly washed ashore, but should not be collected because their colors quickly fade—even before they are dry.

The daintiest and most colorful flora and fauna are found along the Pacific coast from southern California to the northern part of South America. Most of them grow attached to rocks and reefs, but often they are loosened during storms and washed ashore. These gifts of the sea—plants, corals, and shells —are the materials we use in underwater pictures.

Some sea plants resemble terrestrial forms except for being small. A lacy black one that floats in on the shores of the Middle Atlantic states has curved branches studded with small nodes that suggest fine tatting. Picked up on paper from the water, it suggests a modern painting. Sargassum and a related plant which I have not been able to identify are plentiful on beaches of the Bahama Islands, and they even drift as far as Florida. They have miniature fernlike leaves amply supplied with rounded capsules or bladders that harden when they dry. The capsules of fresh plants are light tan, but when they have hardened they are dark brown. Short tan densely feathered clusters find their way to both the east and west coasts of Florida. A white clustered form, composed of many small rounded pieces, suggests overlapping platelets. Some are found at the southern end of Fort Lauderdale, but they are abundant on the less populated beaches of other off-shore islands farther north.

On New Jersey beaches, long, slender, light-tan fernlike seaweeds are found, and an open lacy kind with slender black segments. Both are very effective in undersea pictures.

Sea fauna and flora along the Pacific Coast differ from Atlantic Coast species in formation, design, and color and the most gaily colored ones are found from San Diego and the coastal islands to the southern tip of Lower California, Mexico. Fragments of sea fans and other formations are sometimes washed ashore, but if whole clusters are wanted they have to be chiseled from the rocks where they grow. The only way to reach the beds is by boat, or by jeep over natural terrain from Agua Caliente southward or from La Paz to the ocean, a distance of fifty miles.

Among sea fans found in this area are yellow ones with tiny red spots, composed of medium large to small fans in a single cluster. (These are used medicinally in Mexico to stem hemorrhages.) A smaller and finer coral cluster is colored blood red. Another form reminds one of interlocked antlers: each slender segment shades alternately from coral to white. Another slender form consists of a cluster of branched segments that suggest needle-point lace.

At Agua Caliente small red, or red and pink, plants are washed up on the beach. Bunches of them are tossed among

pebbles well up the inclined slope. Except that they are bright-
ly colored, they resemble terrestrial ferns. Then in the centers
of some there are tiny balls that suggest flower buds.

PICTURES WITH SEAWEEDS

When plants are collected from the sea they dry out quickly.
To soften them, soak them in water. When they have become
pliant, remove each specimen separately by slipping a large
sheet of waterproof paper under it and lifting it from the water.
This technique enables it to retain its underwater appearance.
Now flatten it and shape it to conform to the design of the
picture you plan to make, adding whatever accessory growths
you need.

Imaginary flower gardens can be created with seaweeds by
selecting forms in imitation of leaves, flowers, and buds. One
red alga from the coast of southern California closely resembles a pinnate leaf of a flowering plant.

Compositions designed in imitation of underwater scenes
are especially natural-looking when they give the effect of the
water flowing from one side to the other. The unattached end
of a slender seaweed sometimes appears fringed as it moves
with waves or current. To simulate this movement gives a seaweed picture life because it recalls natural situations.

As long as the seaweeds remain moist, they can be ma-
nipulated to create the scene one has in mind. When completed, let the plants and background paper dry together.
When thoroughly dry, the composition can be framed.

USING ANIMALS FROM THE SEA

When sea fans and other growths have been collected to create
a scene, they first need to be washed to remove sand and fragments of other foreign matter. As soon as they dry they will curl,
but sea fans need only to be rinsed and flattened to keep them
in proper shape. Curled growths can be kept in a box until it
is convenient to soak them in water. When they become soft

enough to shape, spread them out and place them between blotters to dry.

Shell animals are often attached to the stems of sea fans and other fauna. Also on the sea bottom, or swimming above it, are sand dollars, starfish, spiny sea urchins, and sea horses. Underwater pictures can feature these.

Underwater scenes in three dimensions can be designed on Specimen Riker Mounts measuring twelve by sixteen inches. Each shallow box contains two layers of cotton. The top layer is of fine quality, pure white, and covered with a glass top. Take out the white cotton, place it on a board, and either draw the two together through liquid-bluing water or sprinkle the cotton generously with it. The first method will color the cotton evenly; the second will leave streaks and blotches which suggest water in motion. Slant the board to allow the excess water to drain off, then lay a towel over the cotton and invert the board. When all excess water has been removed, turn the cotton onto towels to dry. (Do not handle wet cotton by itself or it will pull apart.) Cover it lightly with a piece of clean paper to prevent bleaching and place it in an airy sunny place to dry. Another way to dry it is to lay it on a towel-covered cookie sheet and place it on a radiator or in front of an electric fan.

When the cotton is thoroughly dry, replace it in the box, and arrange the sea flora and fauna you have collected in a pleasing design. (Designs can be made for long or broad pictures.) Overlay some pieces, if necessary. Most of the components will adhere to the cotton, so that you can stand the picture upright to study your design and make any changes that seem necessary to improve it. Next, embellish the picture with shells. Only those that are very smooth will need to be glued to keep them from slipping out of place.

A flower garden under water is usually designed for a picture that is to hang lengthwise. Strands of colored gorgonia, or gracefully bent black ones from which the colorful parts have been eroded by the action of waves and sand, are used for stems. Flower spikes are made by gluing small snails in a pendulous position at intervals along the stem. Single valves of shells are used for this same purpose. The spikes, of various lengths, arise from the bottom and lower sides of a sea fan, and extend up and across the center of the picture. At the base are pieces of dark seaweeds and a few large, colorful shells.

When the picture is finished, replace the glass top and fasten the two parts of the box together with the four pins that were in it originally. To protect the picture from dust and dampness, seal it with gummed tape, or masking tape, from the sides to the underside. Slit the tape at the corners so that it will overlap smoothly.

Picture frames at least two inches wide are better for this art form than narrow ones. Those that are unpainted can be rubbed with sea-green oil paint and streaked with blue to extend the color of the water. Faint tints of dominant shells are often rubbed in here and there over the original paint after it has dried. At the mitered corners of the frame and in the crevices of ridges, use a camel's hair brush to apply the paint. Smooth and blend in any excess paint with a small piece of turkish toweling.

13 MONTAGES AND OTHER DECORATIONS

Shells can be used decoratively in many ways other than those we have described so far—for montage and découpage, for three-panel screens, for ornamenting boxes, mirrors, and purses, and for jewelry. Once you have become absorbed in shell art, you will probably develop ideas of your own.

MONTAGES

In a montage, or three-dimensional panel, shells are mounted high enough to cast a shadow. Usually these arrangements are not glassed, but sometimes they are put in deep shadow boxes.

A montage can be of any size and can be designed to harmonize with the décor of a room. It can be hung for either height or width. The more usual arrangements are seascapes and beach scenes. Shell fanciers prefer to use natural-colored shells that range from white to vivid colors, or are marked with contrasting hues. In addition, they make effective use of shells of intricate sculpture, and contrasting shapes and sizes. The background is generally a panel of fiber glass or wood.

If the focal point of the design is planned for the center of the arrangement, start there with the largest shells. Super-

impose a large univalve on a somewhat larger half of a bivalve, then build around these with shells of decreasing size
from top to bottom and from side to side. To suggest depth,
a partially opened bivalve can be glued between other shells.
If the best color is on the inside of the shell, let it be open
rather wide. The hinges are glued to the panel to project the
shells forward.

After the two large shells have been glued into position, it
is advisable to attach other shells tentatively with re-usable
plastic. Knead a small piece into a ball and press it firmly onto
the fiber glass, and then gently press a shell onto the plastic
ball. When a pleasing design has been found, remove in turn
each shell and its plastic fastening and put a piece of gluey
cotton in the same place and on it press the shell. Strands of
gorgonia with intermittent small, inconspicuous shells, brittle
starfish, or other delicately colored subjects will taper the picture and focus the eyes on its center. If the focal point is to
be at one side, an interesting composition can be made to suggest a rolling or graded beach. Small shells can be scattered
along a descending line. On a wooden panel, shells ranging
from white to brown are most effective.

More unusual than beach scenes are floral pictures of
more or less oriental or tropical design. Other pictures suggest
flower gardens or bouquets. All shell flowers used in this way
are made individually and then glued on the panel.

When a panel has been finished, spray the shells lightly
with clear plastic. They can then be easily rinsed to remove
accumulations of dust.

The interior color of univalves varies widely. To reveal
the hidden color they are sometimes sliced by professionals
with a diamond saw. The slices may be thick or thin, cut from
large or small shells, and they can be used in many ways. A
very artistic panel seen in a Florida shell supply house was
decorated with thickly sliced rose murex shells from Mexico.
The interior of these shells is a beautiful rosy-pink, and the
lacy edges of the shells add further beauty to the ensemble.
Thin slices of smaller shells are popular for making shell
jewelry.

THREE-PANEL SCREENS

Three-panel screens of various sizes, made of glass or fiber glass, are useful as well as decorative. Flat shells, such as Philippine window shells, the flat valves of certain scallops, and others, are arranged in a design on each panel. Surrounding the shells are flattened specimens of fine sea plants and flat pieces of others cut from slightly thicker, densely clustered forms. A rough coat of liquid plastic brushed over the design binds it permanently to the panel. Small screens are especially suited for counters of any kind to obstruct undesirable views. Being translucent, they do not altogether exclude light.

DÉCOUPAGE

Shell découpage usually consists of an assemblage of leaves and stems cut from figured wallpaper, flower magazines, or catalogues, and shells or sections cut from them. If an arrangement is made in the form of a bouquet, a large scallop or any other reasonably flat shell, or a large cut shell, can represent a container. Such arrangements are always covered with glass to protect the paper.

Flowers are suggested by gluing a few shell petals or cut shells directly on a board or panel. Individual shells and paper leaves and stems are interspersed among them. Paste is applied only to the center of leaves so that their edges will curl slightly. Flowers are often highly imaginative and the closest approach to a real one is a cluster of Queen Anne's lace composed of minute shells and furnished with paper stems and foliage. These flowers lie flat and several of them placed at the sides of a bouquet give it an airy gracefulness.

FLOWER PICTURES

A shell enthusiast in the Middle West makes many kinds of artistic shell-flower pictures. Some are on a velvet background; others are on glass painted green underneath to suggest shimmering sea water. She often uses antique oval frames fitted with concave glass. Natural-colored shells are mainly used for flowers and foliage. In shallow pictures, flower custers of Queen Anne's lace are particularly charming because of their three-dimensional effect. For making them she uses tiny lilac shells in natural color, gluing them directly to the background. In some sections of a cluster she superimposes additional shells of the same kind so that the arrangement will not be flat.

Small round shells of natural-colored purple and violet hues do not exist. Dyed shells are therefore used in these pictures for making lilacs. Shells for flowers of varying shades are glued directly to the background and additional shells of the same color are superimposed throughout the center to provide a third dimension. Containers are suggested by slightly convex or flat shells of proper size, glued to the base of the picture.

For other types of pictures made with marine life forms, see Chapter Eleven.

GLASS FISH BOWL WITH SEA FAUNA

By using corals and other materials washed up on the shore, you can capture a bit of the sea in a glass fish bowl. Select an attractive cluster of sea fans and attach it off center to the bottom of the bowl with floral clay. Add a group of sea whips—the tips—in the same way. Now cover the bottom of the bowl with sand, making sure that the clay is completely hidden.

Arrange on the sand, to form the base of your picture, any or all of the following items: a small sea urchin, a small starfish, a few shells, a cured cowfish. The cowfish is suitable because of its flat base. In the middle part of the picture, glue a cured needlefish so that it seems to be swimming between sections of the sea fan cluster.

Other forms that can be used are winged oysters and jewelboxes (*Chama* species), which normally attach themselves to the stems of sea feathers and other waving corals. Glue them to a strip of *Gorgonia*. At a higher level attach a flamingo tongue to a sea fan. Or glue a sea horse, head up, to a piece of *Gorgonia*. Sea horses swim in an upright position and rest with their tails curled around any waving coral formation. They—or any seemingly live shells—can be arranged at various levels to achieve an artistic effect.

MIRRORS, BOXES, AND OTHER ITEMS

Both framed and unframed mirrors are sometimes encrusted with scallop shells, usually white and lacquered. Others are decorated with shells and coral, arranged alternately. They are very attractive and greatly admired. Shell-trimmed purses can be elaborately beautiful—and expensive. Less costly ones with shell decorations are quickly made and are popular commercial items. Trays of various sizes and shapes, with small or reasonably flat shells arranged on velvet and covered with glass, are in demand too.

Attractive place cards and tallies, decorated with very small dyed shells and green pen drawings of leaves and stems are also made. Boxes for tissues, powder, pills, and other commodities are decorated with whole or cut shells, pieces of coral, and irregular pieces of pearly Mississippi River clams left after the cutting of buttons for which these shells are reserved. Individual shells are also used as ash and pin trays, with small shells decorating their hinges. For children there are dolls, animals, and airplanes made of shells.

It would be unthinkable to disrupt a collection to make any of the decorations we have described, but many cartons of good shells are stored every year in attics and garages and then forgotten. They could be cleaned to bring out their lovely colors and used in ways that give pleasure to all.

14 SHELL ANIMALS AND DOLLS

ANIMALS

Shell animals never fail to delight children, and some of them are so simple that they can make them themselves. Pipe cleaners, cotton, shell glue, toothpicks, cutting pliers, and suitable shells are all that is needed to construct them.

MOUSE. Boat-shells are perfect for mice. They come in various shades of brown, up to three inches in length, and the pointed ends of some of them are curved slightly so that the head can be in different positions. A single shell makes the body and head. Glue a coquina on either side of the pointed end for ears. Add two small coquinas cup side down for the forelegs. The blunt end should be toward the front and about half of the shell under the body. Paint in two beady eyes. Make a two-inch tail with a piece of rubber band. Glue it on at the back and snip it with sharp scissors so that it narrows to a point.

COW. For a cow, use a pair of turkey-wing shells. Pack the hollows with cotton and add pipe cleaner legs. Glue and press them all together with the hinged part of the shells at the top. Glue another length of pipe cleaner at the top; it should extend from the center of the head to the tip of the tail. Fill with gluey cotton and press into place at the front a pair of bulged kitten's paws for a head. Paint in the eyes. If desired, the tail and legs can be painted brown. Small round snails, glued to the ends of the legs, serve as hoofs.

TURTLE.   A turtle is also easy to make. Use a good-sized cowrie shell for the body. Along the opening under it, glue a length of pipe cleaner so that it extends through the rounded end for a neck and head. Glue two more pieces of pipe cleaner across the shell from one side to the other to make the legs. Between the body and the head, leave about a quarter of an inch of the pipe cleaner bare for a neck. (The lengths of pipe cleaner used will depend upon the size of the shell.) For a head, glue a ring cowrie flat along the groove onto the pipe cleaner. Use the same kind of shells for the feet, gluing them in the same way. Paint in two black eyes and paint the neck.

SWAN.   To make a swan, first bend a length of pipe cleaner into the shape of an elongated and reversed letter S. Glue one end under a King's crown shell at the place where it opens and tilt the pointed apex end slightly upward. For a resting swan, legs are not needed. If the swan is to stand, glue two pieces of pipe cleaner into the aperture of the shell—not too far from the neck—for the legs. To the end of each leg, glue a very small cerith, coquina, or auger shell for a foot. For a head, glue a pair of coquinas together, with their hinges up, over the pipe cleaner. Use a small dark auger shell for the beak, the slender point at the tip.

LAMB.   To make a woolly lamb, first wrap gluey cotton around a length of pipe cleaner and mold a thin body, allowing a short end to project for a stubby tail and about a quarter of an inch at the other end for attaching the head. Glue four short lengths of pipe cleaner to the underside of the body for legs. Now fill out the body of the lamb by gluing small white cup shells (three-eighths to one-quarter of an inch) to the cotton. Start at the neck with the smaller shells, gluing them cup side up with the hinges toward the rear. Using shells progressively larger, glue on following rows, always overlapping the hinges. Continue to the last row, at the tail. This last row should be made of smaller shells. Glue one-eighth of an inch cup shells to the tail, cup side up. Cover the legs with the same tiny shells, cup side up, with the hinges toward the feet. For feet use small round white shells, such as pikakis. The head is made of a pair of light-colored kitten's paws glued together. Dot in black eyes.

DOLLS

Dolls of almost any type can be made out of shells. In addition to a varied shell collection, you will need pipe cleaners, pliers, cotton, shell glue, and painted faces with blonde, brown, black, or red hair. Among shells that you will need for the head are matching shells of proper size and shape for the face and the back of the head, and one-eighth- to one-quarter-inch cup shells, dyed to match the hair on the forehead, for the back of the head. For the upper part of the body, you will need two matching lucinas.

A COLONIAL DOLL.   A colonial doll five inches high has a floor-length skirt made of green keyhole limpets, which enables it to stand erect. For the foundation use two pipe cleaners, one for the body and one for the arms. The doll's skirt will be three inches long, the upper part of body one inch and the head one inch.

Make a one-inch loop at the end of a piece of pipe cleaner five inches long and put the straight end through the largest limpet and level it. Put a spot of glue on the top of the shell to hold it fast. Add other shells, which may be of progressively smaller size and not necessarily level, using a little glue at the top of each. Continue up to the waistline. Put some glue and cotton in the hollow part of the two lucinas which are to form the upper body and place the length of pipe cleaner that is to form the arms across one of them, a half inch above the waistline. Add more glue and press the shells together. When the shells are completely dry, bend the arms at the shoulders and elbows so that the ends are brought together at the waist.

To make the head, put glue and cotton into the hollows of the face shell and the shell for the back of the head. Add more glue and press them together on the remaining part of the pipe cleaner. When the head is dry, glue cup shells to the back for hair. If the little shells are glued with the hollow side up, the hair will look curly. If the hollow side is down, wavy hair is suggested. Add the painted face.

Hands cannot be simulated. Glue in a small rose or a bouquet at the ends of the arms to conceal the lack of them. Egg cases of murex come in clusters, some cream-colored, some pink-tinged. Snip off a rounded section to use for a bouquet.

AN EASIER DOLL.   A doll that is easier to make has a wide skirt made of two white bay scallops. Add cotton packing half way down them from the waistline, mold it to fit the inner contour of the two shells, and bind them together. Make sure the shells are level so that the doll will stand erect. Complete the doll by following the directions given for the colonial doll.

PERIOD DOLLS.   Fancy and period dolls with shoes are more detailed than the two we have described and require a little more time. They can be as high as six inches. The basic instructions are similar to those given, but the end of the pipe cleaner that holds the skirt is not looped and must be molded with cotton to conform to the contour of the desired style. If the skirt is to be above the floor level, an extra length of pipe cleaner must be twisted into place so that there will be two legs, and shoes must be contrived. When completed, these dolls must be glued to a base, such as a clam shell.

For a petal skirt that flares at the bottom, use yellow, white, or orange jingle shells with the bulged side down. Begin at the bottom of the skirt and be sure to lap each following row over the hinges of the previous row. Large rose petal shells can be used for a skirt in this same way. For a fine lacy ruffling skirt, use half-inch white cup shells (or dyed cup shells), gluing them into place with the cup side down. For a hoop skirt or hobble skirt, glue the shells cup side down and make the skirt narrower at the bottom. Skirts with bustles are made over a hand-molded base.

If a collar is desired, it can be provided by slipping a keyhole limpet over the pipe cleaner at the top. A large one will extend over the shoulders. Or a row of small matching shells can be glued around the body at the shoulders. Among those that are suitable are small calico pectens. (Lavender ones are found abundantly on the bay side of Sanibel Island in Florida.)

To make the feet of the doll, turn the ends of the leg wires forward one-eighth of an inch and glue them flat to the base. Then glue a coquina shell cup side down on the foot portion with the point forward.

15 SHELL JEWELRY

Shell jewelry is a dainty accessory, especially suitable for wear with pastel summer clothing. It is not difficult to make and so inexpensive that you can easily provide an assortment of designs and colors to harmonize with different costumes.

Many shell dealers sell beginner's kits, including directions for constructing pins, earrings, and other items, and list in their catalogues the many, many shells that are suitable for this use. After a little practice, you will probably be making your own designs.

The materials needed for making shell jewelry are very simple. For brooches and earrings you will need plastic or mother-of-pearl foundation disks of different shapes and sizes, pins, ear wires, shell glue, cotton, toothpicks, and tweezers.

Small whole shells are often used in making various items, but cut shells are more popular because of their unusual shapes and the interest provided by contrasting interior and exterior colors. The shape of the jewelry will depend upon the style of cut. There are half cuts, slices, top cuts, lengthwise cuts to which a small inner section remains attached, swirls that are usually interlaced, and mother-of-pearl pendants that are pierced for the insertion of a small metal ring. By manipulating these various pieces, interesting results can be obtained.

Brooches made on plastic and mother-of-pearl disks require slightly different techniques. For either, first select a disk of the desired size and shape and assemble all the shells and other materials to be used. If a plastic disk is to be covered completely with small shells, spread a thin layer of shell glue over it. On top of this apply a very thin layer of cotton and then add another thin layer of glue. Apply the shells with the aid of tweezers and maneuver them into place with a toothpick. The cotton aids in binding the shells securely to the disk.

Whole cocoa cockles or half cuts of green limpits provide a flowerlike design when glued on round disks. The centers can be ornamented with seed pearls or small rhinestones of matching color. Juvenile, yellow-dyed whelks, and dyed mustard seeds can also be used. Remember to waterproof all dyed shells and other materials by coating them with lacquer before you glue them into place.

If you are using mother-of-pearl disks as foundations, do not cover them with cotton. Put a little glue on each shell, using a toothpick, and cement it to the disk. The beauty of open-cut shells is enhanced by the mother-of-pearl that shows through the openings. For lengthening a pin or earring, add a mother-of-pearl bangle. Slip a ring through the pierced hole and glue the ring to the disk under a shell.

Dyed fish scales are also used in making jewelry, notably for flower forms. In this case the scales are not usually lacquered, because after a while the lacquer turns yellow and dulls the colors of the scales. A disadvantage here is that the unlacquered jewelry cannot be washed or cleaned.

Ideal for making a carnation for a boutonnière are red or pink bonefish scales, which have dentate edges. Roll a small ball of cotton in the palms of your hands, put a spot of glue under it, and place it on a sheet of oiled glass or plastic. The glue will hold it in place while you work. Pat the cotton down so that it is as thick as a carnation at the top, then start the flower at the bottom of the ball, using the largest scales. Put a little glue on the base of a petal and attach it to the bottom of the cotton, bending it slightly outward. Complete the bottom row. Add another row of petals inside of the bottom row, keeping it on the same level. When the two bottom rows of scales are in place, go to the top of the flower and glue in the smallest scales, again keeping them on the same level. Glue more scales around and around, still maintaining a uniform level, until the flower has been filled in completely. Let the finished carnation dry thoroughly, then glue it to a disk.

For a rose use buffalo-fish or carp scales. Some of these curl slightly, as rose petals do, adding to the grace of the flower. Select a round disk of appropriate size and spread it with a thin coating of glue, then with a flat layer of cotton. Glue in the largest scales at the base of the flower, keeping them reasonably flat. Add smaller scales. An open rose is not dense so not many rows are needed. Finish the center with tiny scales. A rose of this form displays the curl of the scale petals to advantage.

If you want to use leaves with the flowers, green-dyed scales can be cut to suitable size or you can use small green garfish scales for roses. Put a little dab of glue under them and tuck them beneath the flower. Slender cuts from other scales can be used for carnation leaves.

By following these general instructions, and consulting the directions given for flowers used in bouquets, you can make brooches and earrings, bracelets, pendants, and boutonnières featuring many additional species.

16 NEW FLOWERS, NEW METHODS

A few easier methods have recently been devised for making certain shell flowers.

DAHLIA. The dahlia from coquina shells was made on a plastic disk (see page 65). However, you can achieve the same result with cotton, using the following technique. Fashion a one-inch ball of cotton. Put glue on the point of the shell and poke it into the cotton ball. Continue this procedure until you have formed a flat, round row of shells around the bottom of the cotton ball. Allow it to dry for a few minutes. Add one additional row of shells just above, so that the bottom row of shells shows slightly below. For all additional rows, affix glue to the hinge edge of the shell and poke it into the cotton in a more upright position, using shells of decreasing size as you approach the top of the flower.

RANUNCULUS. The delicate flowers in white and shades of yellow and orange are made by using convex-shaped *Anomia simplex*, commonly known as jingle shell. Carefully remove all irregularities with scissors. On top of a three-quarter-inch ball of cotton glue two- to two-and-a-half-inch jingles. Glue larger overlapping shells around them. Continue with another row of one-inch shells.

To make a rounded flower of shells one-and-a-quarter-inch

long, begin with shells one-half-inch long, on a three-quarter-inch ball. Continue with increasingly larger shells, always overlapping, until the final or outside row of shells measures one-and-a-quarter-inch long. Be certain that all shells are level or almost level at the top. Trim carefully, with scissors, any thick, bulky or irregular base.

BABY ROSE.   Use shell glue to hold together one-eighth- to three-sixteenths-inch-long white cups—juvenile shells of several species which resemble each other. When dry and firm, turn flower upside down and glue about five shells concave side down, with the hinges forming the outer edge. The hinge ends will resemble curved petals. To make a shaded pink and white baby rose, follow the directions given for making a baby rose. The pink color will be at the base of the budlike formation and the hinge ends of the shells will give the pink color.

MINIATURE ROSE.   Use a piece of pliable plastic material as a working area. Dip the base of the shell known as Job's tears into white glue. Affix the glued shell bases to the pliable plastic in a circle, leaving the center (about three quarters of an inch) open. Form a small ring of shells, leaving a proportionately smaller open circle. Allow to dry. Glue the smaller ring into the center of the larger one. Then, in the center of the smaller circle of shells, glue some additional shells to form a budlike cluster. When dry, shell rings and clusters can be removed easily by using a flat knife or by flexing the plastic. To make a stem, turn the dry flower upside down. Cut a one- to two-inch piece of wrapped green wire. Dip one end in white glue and attach to the center of the base of the flower.

BIBLIOGRAPHY

Abbott, R. Tucker. *American Seashells*. D. Van Nostrand, Princeton, 1955.

_____ *Introducing Seashells*. D. Van Nostrand, Princeton, 1955.

_____ *Sea Shells of the World*. Golden Press, New York, 1962.

Allan, Joyce. *Australian Shells*. Griffen Press, Adelaide. Rev. ed., 1959.

Bailey, L. H. *Standard Cyclopedia of Horticulture*. 3 vols. Macmillan, New York, 1933.

Bailey, L. H. and Ethel Zoe Bailey. *Hortus* Second. Macmillan, New York, 1939.

Bousefield, F. L. *Canadian Sea Shells*. Canadian Museum of Canada, 1960.

Cox, Ian (Ed.) *The Scallop*, Studies of a Shell and its Influence on Human Kind. Shell Transport and Trading Co., 135 pp., pamphlet, London, 1957.

Grant, John. *Manual of Heraldry*. Edinburgh, 1904.

Jacobson, Morris K. and William K. Emerson. *Shells of the New York City Area from Cape Cod to Cape May*. Argonaut Books, Larchmont, N.Y., 1961. Dover reprint

Kira, Tetsuaki. *Colored Illustrations of Japanese Shells*, 71 color plates. Hoikusha, Osaka, 2nd. ed., 1960.

Krauss, Helen K. *Geraniums for Home and Garden*, Macmillan, New York, 1955.

Olsson, Axel and Anne Harbison. *Pliocene Mollusca of Southern Florida*. The Academy of Natural Sciences, Philadelphia. (Monograph 8), 1953.

Platt, Rutherford. "Shells Take You over World Horizons," in *National Geographic Magazine*, July 1949.

Smith, F. G. Walton (Ed.) *Sea Frontiers*. Magazine of the International Oceanographic Foundation. Paper-bound quarterly. Miami.

Sterns, Mabel (Ed.) *Shells and their Neighbors*. Periodical, October 1960 issue, Redlands, Calif.

Taylor, Norman (Ed.) *Taylor's Encyclopedia of Gardening*. Houghton Mifflin, Boston, 1961.

Verrill, A. Hyatt. *The Shell Collector's Handbook*. Putnam, New York, 1950.

Vilas, C. N. and N. R. *Florida Marine Shells*. Bobbs-Merrill, Indianapolis, 1952.

Warmke, Germaine and R. Tucker Abbott. *Caribbean Seashells*. Livingston Publishing Co., Narbeth, Pennsylvania, 1961. Dover reprint

Webb, Walter F. *Recent Mollusca from all Parts of the World*. Author, St. Petersburg 3, Florida. 4th ed., n. d.

Zieber, Eugene. *Heraldry in America*. Published privately, Bailey, Banks, and Biddle, Philadelphia, 1909.

INDEX

A CATALOGUE OF
SELECTED DOVER BOOKS
IN ALL FIELDS OF INTEREST

A CATALOGUE OF SELECTED DOVER
BOOKS IN ALL FIELDS OF INTEREST

CONDITIONED REFLEXES, Ivan P. Pavlov. Full translation of most complete statement of Pavlov's work; cerebral damage, conditioned reflex, experiments with dogs, sleep, similar topics of great importance. 430pp. 5⅜ x 8½.   60614-7 Pa. $4.50

NOTES ON NURSING: WHAT IT IS, AND WHAT IT IS NOT, Florence Nightingale. Outspoken writings by founder of modern nursing. When first published (1860) it played an important role in much needed revolution in nursing. Still stimulating. 140pp. 5⅜ x 8½.   22340-X Pa. $2.50

HARTER'S PICTURE ARCHIVE FOR COLLAGE AND ILLUSTRATION, Jim Harter. Over 300 authentic, rare 19th-century engravings selected by noted collagist for artists, designers, decoupeurs, etc. Machines, people, animals, etc., printed one side of page. 25 scene plates for backgrounds. 6 collages by Harter, Satty, Singer, Evans. Introduction. 192pp. 8⅞ x 11¾.   23659-5 Pa. $5.00

MANUAL OF TRADITIONAL WOOD CARVING, edited by Paul N. Hasluck. Possibly the best book in English on the craft of wood carving. Practical instructions, along with 1,146 working drawings and photographic illustrations. Formerly titled *Cassell's Wood Carving*. 576pp. 6½ x 9¼.
23489-4 Pa. $7.95

THE PRINCIPLES AND PRACTICE OF HAND OR SIMPLE TURNING, John Jacob Holtzapffel. Full coverage of basic lathe techniques—history and development, special apparatus, softwood turning, hardwood turning, metal turning. Many projects—billiard ball, works formed within a sphere, egg cups, ash trays, vases, jardiniers, others—included. 1881 edition. 800 illustrations. 592pp. 6⅛ x 9¼.   23365-0 Clothbd. $15.00

THE JOY OF HANDWEAVING, Osma Tod. Only book you need for hand weaving. Fundamentals, threads, weaves, plus numerous projects for small board-loom, two-harness, tapestry, laid-in, four-harness weaving and more. Over 160 illustrations. 2nd revised edition. 352pp. 6½ x 9¼.
23458-4 Pa. $5.00

THE BOOK OF WOOD CARVING, Charles Marshall Sayers. Still finest book for beginning student in wood sculpture. Noted teacher, craftsman discusses fundamentals, technique; gives 34 designs, over 34 projects for panels, bookends, mirrors, etc. "Absolutely first-rate"—E. J. Tangerman. 33 photos. 118pp. 7¾ x 10⅝.   23654-4 Pa. $3.00

DRAWINGS OF WILLIAM BLAKE, William Blake. 92 plates from Book of Job, *Divine Comedy, Paradise Lost,* visionary heads, mythological figures, Laocoon, etc. Selection, introduction, commentary by Sir Geoffrey Keynes. 178pp. 8⅛ x 11.   22303-5 Pa. $4.00

ENGRAVINGS OF HOGARTH, William Hogarth. 101 of Hogarth's greatest works: *Rake's Progress, Harlot's Progress, Illustrations for Hudibras, Before and After, Beer Street and Gin Lane,* many more. Full commentary. 256pp. 11 x 13¾.   22479-1 Pa. $7.95

DAUMIER: 120 GREAT LITHOGRAPHS, Honore Daumier. Wide-ranging collection of lithographs by the greatest caricaturist of the 19th century. Concentrates on eternally popular series on lawyers, on married life, on liberated women, etc. Selection, introduction, and notes on plates by Charles F. Ramus. Total of 158pp. 9⅜ x 12¼.   23512-2 Pa. $5.50

DRAWINGS OF MUCHA, Alphonse Maria Mucha. Work reveals drafts-man of highest caliber: studies for famous posters and paintings, render-ings for book illustrations and ads, etc. 70 works, 9 in color; including 6 items not drawings. Introduction. List of illustrations. 72pp. 9⅜ x 12¼. (Available in U.S. only)   23672-2 Pa. $4.00

GIOVANNI BATTISTA PIRANESI: DRAWINGS IN THE PIERPONT MORGAN LIBRARY, Giovanni Battista Piranesi. For first time ever all of Morgan Library's collection, world's largest. 167 illustrations of rare Piranesi drawings—archeological, architectural, decorative and visionary. Essay, detailed list of drawings, chronology, captions. Edited by Felice Stampfle. 144pp. 9⅜ x 12¼.   23714-1 Pa. $7.50

NEW YORK ETCHINGS (1905-1949), John Sloan. All of important American artist's N.Y. life etchings. 67 works include some of his best art; also lively historical record—Greenwich Village, tenement scenes. Edited by Sloan's widow. Introduction and captions. 79pp. 8⅜ x 11¼.
23651-X Pa. $4.00

CHINESE PAINTING AND CALLIGRAPHY: A PICTORIAL SURVEY, Wan-go Weng. 69 fine examples from John M. Crawford's matchless private collection: landscapes, birds, flowers, human figures, etc., plus calligraphy. Every basic form included: hanging scrolls, handscrolls, album leaves, fans, etc. 109 illustrations. Introduction. Captions. 192pp. 8⅞ x 11¾.
23707-9 Pa. $7.95

DRAWINGS OF REMBRANDT, edited by Seymour Slive. Updated Lipp-mann, Hofstede de Groot edition, with definitive scholarly apparatus. All portraits, biblical sketches, landscapes, nudes, Oriental figures, classical studies, together with selection of work by followers. 550 illustrations. Total of 630pp. 9⅛ x 12¼.   21485-0, 21486-9 Pa., Two-vol. set $15.00

THE DISASTERS OF WAR, Francisco Goya. 83 etchings record horrors of Napoleonic wars in Spain and war in general. Reprint of 1st edition, plus 3 additional plates. Introduction by Philip Hofer. 97pp. 9⅜ x 8¼.
21872-4 Pa. $3.75

THE EARLY WORK OF AUBREY BEARDSLEY, Aubrey Beardsley. 157 plates, 2 in color: *Manon Lescaut, Madame Bovary, Morte Darthur, Salome,* other. Introduction by H. Marillier. 182pp. 8⅛ x 11. 21816-3 Pa. $4.50

THE LATER WORK OF AUBREY BEARDSLEY, Aubrey Beardsley. Exotic masterpieces of full maturity: *Venus and Tannhauser, Lysistrata, Rape of the Lock, Volpone,* Savoy material, etc. 174 plates, 2 in color. 186pp. 8⅛ x 11. 21817-1 Pa. $4.50

THOMAS NAST'S CHRISTMAS DRAWINGS, Thomas Nast. Almost all Christmas drawings by creator of image of Santa Claus as we know it, and one of America's foremost illustrators and political cartoonists. 66 illustrations. 3 illustrations in color on covers. 96pp. 8⅜ x 11¼.
23660-9 Pa. $3.50

THE DORÉ ILLUSTRATIONS FOR DANTE'S DIVINE COMEDY, Gustave Doré. All 135 plates from Inferno, Purgatory, Paradise; fantastic tortures, infernal landscapes, celestial wonders. Each plate with appropriate (translated) verses. 141pp. 9 x 12. 23231-X Pa. $4.50

DORÉ'S ILLUSTRATIONS FOR RABELAIS, Gustave Doré. 252 striking illustrations of *Gargantua and Pantagruel* books by foremost 19th-century illustrator. Including 60 plates, 192 delightful smaller illustrations. 153pp. 9 x 12. 23656-0 Pa. $5.00

LONDON: A PILGRIMAGE, Gustave Doré, Blanchard Jerrold. Squalor, riches, misery, beauty of mid-Victorian metropolis; 55 wonderful plates, 125 other illustrations, full social, cultural text by Jerrold. 191pp. of text. 9⅜ x 12¼. 22306-X Pa. $6.00

THE RIME OF THE ANCIENT MARINER, Gustave Doré, S. T. Coleridge. Dore's finest work, 34 plates capture moods, subtleties of poem. Full text. Introduction by Millicent Rose. 77pp. 9¼ x 12. 22305-1 Pa. $3.50

THE DORE BIBLE ILLUSTRATIONS, Gustave Doré. All wonderful, detailed plates: Adam and Eve, Flood, Babylon, Life of Jesus, etc. Brief King James text with each plate. Introduction by Millicent Rose. 241 plates. 241pp. 9 x 12. 23004-X Pa. $6.00

THE COMPLETE ENGRAVINGS, ETCHINGS AND DRYPOINTS OF ALBRECHT DURER. "Knight, Death and Devil"; "Melencolia," and more—all Dürer's known works in all three media, including 6 works formerly attributed to him. 120 plates. 235pp. 8⅜ x 11¼.
22851-7 Pa. $6.50

MAXIMILIAN'S TRIUMPHAL ARCH, Albrecht Dürer and others. Incredible monument of woodcut art: 8 foot high elaborate arch—heraldic figures, humans, battle scenes, fantastic elements—that you can assemble yourself. Printed on one side, layout for assembly. 143pp. 11 x 16.
21451-6 Pa. $5.00

THE COMPLETE WOODCUTS OF ALBRECHT DURER, edited by Dr. W. Kurth. 346 in all: "Old Testament," "St. Jerome," "Passion," "Life of Virgin," Apocalypse," many others. Introduction by Campbell Dodgson. 285pp. 8½ x 12¼. 21097-9 Pa. $6.95

DRAWINGS OF ALBRECHT DURER, edited by Heinrich Wolfflin. 81 plates show development from youth to full style. Many favorites; many new. Introduction by Alfred Werner. 96pp. 8⅛ x 11. 22352-3 Pa. $5.00

THE HUMAN FIGURE, Albrecht Dürer. Experiments in various techniques—stereometric, progressive proportional, and others. Also life studies that rank among finest ever done. Complete reprinting of *Dresden Sketchbook*. 170 plates. 355pp. 8⅜ x 11¼. 21042-1 Pa. $7.95

OF THE JUST SHAPING OF LETTERS, Albrecht Dürer. Renaissance artist explains design of Roman majuscules by geometry, also Gothic lower and capitals. Grolier Club edition. 43pp. 7⅞ x 10¾ 21306-4 Pa. $3.00

TEN BOOKS ON ARCHITECTURE, Vitruvius. The most important book ever written on architecture. Early Roman aesthetics, technology, classical orders, site selection, all other aspects. Stands behind everything since. Morgan translation. 331pp. 5⅜ x 8½. 20645-9 Pa. $4.00

THE FOUR BOOKS OF ARCHITECTURE, Andrea Palladio. 16th-century classic responsible for Palladian movement and style. Covers classical architectural remains, Renaissance revivals, classical orders, etc. 1738 Ware English edition. Introduction by A. Placzek. 216 plates. 110pp. of text. 9½ x 12¾. 21308-0 Pa. $8.95

HORIZONS, Norman Bel Geddes. Great industrialist stage designer, "father of streamlining," on application of aesthetics to transportation, amusement, architecture, etc. 1932 prophetic account; function, theory, specific projects. 222 illustrations. 312pp. 7⅞ x 10¾. 23514-9 Pa. $6.95

FRANK LLOYD WRIGHT'S FALLINGWATER, Donald Hoffmann. Full, illustrated story of conception and building of Wright's masterwork at Bear Run, Pa. 100 photographs of site, construction, and details of completed structure. 112pp. 9¼ x 10. 23671-4 Pa. $5.00

THE ELEMENTS OF DRAWING, John Ruskin. Timeless classic by great Viltorian; starts with basic ideas, works through more difficult. Many practical exercises. 48 illustrations. Introduction by Lawrence Campbell. 228pp. 5⅜ x 8½. 22730-8 Pa. $2.75

GIST OF ART, John Sloan. Greatest modern American teacher, Art Students League, offers innumerable hints, instructions, guided comments to help you in painting. Not a formal course. 46 illustrations. Introduction by Helen Sloan. 200pp. 5⅜ x 8½. 23435-5 Pa. $3.50

THE ANATOMY OF THE HORSE, George Stubbs. Often considered the
great masterpiece of animal anatomy. Full reproduction of 1766 edition,
plus prospectus; original text and modernized text. 36 plates. Introduction
by Eleanor Garvey. 121pp. 11 x 14¾.   23402-9 Pa. $6.00

BRIDGMAN'S LIFE DRAWING, George B. Bridgman. More than 500
illustrative drawings and text teach you to abstract the body into its major
masses, use light and shade, proportion; as well as specific areas of anatomy,
of which Bridgman is master. 192pp. 6½ x 9¼. (Available in U.S. only)
                                                      22710-3 Pa. $3.00

ART NOUVEAU DESIGNS IN COLOR, Alphonse Mucha, Maurice
Verneuil, Georges Auriol. Full-color reproduction of *Combinaisons orne-
mentales* (c. 1900) by Art Nouveau masters. Floral, animal, geometric,
interlacings, swashes—borders, frames, spots—all incredibly beautiful. 60
plates, hundreds of designs. 9⅜ x 8-1/16.   22885-1 Pa. $4.00

FULL-COLOR FLORAL DESIGNS IN THE ART NOUVEAU STYLE,
E. A. Seguy. 166 motifs, on 40 plates, from *Les fleurs et leurs applications
decoratives* (1902): borders, circular designs, repeats, allovers, "spots."
All in authentic Art Nouveau colors. 48pp. 9⅜ x 12¼.
                                                      23439-8 Pa. $5.00

A DIDEROT PICTORIAL ENCYCLOPEDIA OF TRADES AND IN-
DUSTRY, edited by Charles C. Gillispie. 485 most interesting plates from
the great French Encyclopedia of the 18th century show hundreds of
working figures, artifacts, process, land and cityscapes; glassmaking, paper-
making, metal extraction, construction, weaving, making furniture, clothing,
wigs, dozens of other activities. Plates fully explained. 920pp. 9 x 12.
                      22284-5, 22285-3 Clothbd., Two-vol. set $40.00

HANDBOOK OF EARLY ADVERTISING ART, Clarence P. Hornung.
Largest collection of copyright-free early and antique advertising art ever
compiled. Over 6,000 illustrations, from Franklin's time to the 1890's for
special effects, novelty. Valuable source, almost inexhaustible.
Pictorial Volume. Agriculture, the zodiac, animals, autos, birds, Christmas,
fire engines, flowers, trees, musical instruments, ships, games and sports,
much more. Arranged by subject matter and use. 237 plates. 288pp. 9 x 12.
                                                      20122-8 Clothbd. $13.50

Typographical Volume. Roman and Gothic faces ranging from 10 point to
300 point, "Barnum," German and Old English faces, script, logotypes,
scrolls and flourishes, 1115 ornamental initials, 67 complete alphabets,
more. 310 plates. 320pp. 9 x 12.   20123-6 Clothbd. $15.00

CALLIGRAPHY (CALLIGRAPHIA LATINA), J. G. Schwandner. High
point of 18th-century ornamental calligraphy. Very ornate initials, scrolls,
borders, cherubs, birds, lettered examples. 172pp. 9 x 13.
                                                      20475-8 Pa. $6.00

CATALOGUE OF DOVER BOOKS

ART FORMS IN NATURE, Ernst Haeckel. Multitude of strangely beautiful natural forms: Radiolaria, Foraminifera, jellyfishes, fungi, turtles, bats, etc. All 100 plates of the 19th-century evolutionist's *Kunstformen der Natur* (1904). 100pp. 9⅜ x 12¼. 22987-4 Pa. $4.50

CHILDREN: A PICTORIAL ARCHIVE FROM NINETEENTH-CENTURY SOURCES, edited by Carol Belanger Grafton. 242 rare, copyright-free wood engravings for artists and designers. Widest such selection available. All illustrations in line. 119pp. 8⅜ x 11¼. 23694-3 Pa. $3.50

WOMEN: A PICTORIAL ARCHIVE FROM NINETEENTH-CENTURY SOURCES, edited by Jim Harter. 391 copyright-free wood engravings for artists and designers selected from rare periodicals. Most extensive such collection available. All illustrations in line. 128pp. 9 x 12. 23703-6 Pa. $4.50

ARABIC ART IN COLOR, Prisse d'Avennes. From the greatest ornamentalists of all time—50 plates in color, rarely seen outside the Near East, rich in suggestion and stimulus. Includes 4 plates on covers. 46pp. 9⅜ x 12¼. 23658-7 Pa. $6.00

AUTHENTIC ALGERIAN CARPET DESIGNS AND MOTIFS, edited by June Beveridge. Algerian carpets are world famous. Dozens of geometrical motifs are charted on grids, color-coded, for weavers, needleworkers, craftsmen, designers. 53 illustrations plus 4 in color. 48pp. 8¼ x 11. (Available in U.S. only) 23650-1 Pa. $1.75

DICTIONARY OF AMERICAN PORTRAITS, edited by Hayward and Blanche Cirker. 4000 important Americans, earliest times to 1905, mostly in clear line. Politicians, writers, soldiers, scientists, inventors, industrialists, Indians, Blacks, women, outlaws, etc. Identificatory information. 756pp. 9¼ x 12¾. 21823-6 Clothbd. $40.00

HOW THE OTHER HALF LIVES, Jacob A. Riis. Journalistic record of filth, degradation, upward drive in New York immigrant slums, shops, around 1900. New edition includes 100 original Riis photos, monuments of early photography. 233pp. 10 x 7⅞. 22012-5 Pa. $6.00

NEW YORK IN THE THIRTIES, Berenice Abbott. Noted photographer's fascinating study of city shows new buildings that have become famous and old sights that have disappeared forever. Insightful commentary. 97 photographs. 97pp. 11⅜ x 10. 22967-X Pa. $5.00

MEN AT WORK, Lewis W. Hine. Famous photographic studies of construction workers, railroad men, factory workers and coal miners. New supplement of 18 photos on Empire State building construction. New introduction by Jonathan L. Doherty. Total of 69 photos. 63pp. 8 x 10¾. 23475-4 Pa. $3.00

THE DEPRESSION YEARS AS PHOTOGRAPHED BY ARTHUR ROTH-
STEIN, Arthur Rothstein. First collection devoted entirely to the work of
outstanding 1930s photographer: famous dust storm photo, ragged children,
unemployed, etc. 120 photographs. Captions. 119pp. 9¼ x 10¾.
23590-4 Pa. $5.00

CAMERA WORK: A PICTORIAL GUIDE, Alfred Stieglitz. All 559 illustrations and plates from the most important periodical in the history of
art photography, Camera Work (1903-17). Presented four to a page, reduced in size but still clear, in strict chronological order, with complete
captions. Three indexes. Glossary. Bibliography. 176pp. 8⅜ x 11¼.
23591-2 Pa. $6.95

ALVIN LANGDON COBURN, PHOTOGRAPHER, Alvin L. Coburn. Revealing autobiography by one of greatest photographers of 20th century
gives insider's version of Photo-Secession, plus comments on his own work.
77 photographs by Coburn. Edited by Helmut and Alison Gernsheim.
160pp. 8⅛ x 11.
23685-4 Pa. $6.00

NEW YORK IN THE FORTIES, Andreas Feininger. 162 brilliant photographs by the well-known photographer, formerly with Life magazine, show
commuters, shoppers, Times Square at night, Harlem nightclub, Lower
East Side, etc. Introduction and full captions by John von Hartz. 181pp.
9¼ x 10¾.
23585-8 Pa. $6.00

GREAT NEWS PHOTOS AND THE STORIES BEHIND THEM, John
Faber. Dramatic volume of 140 great news photos, 1855 through 1976,
and revealing stories behind them, with both historical and technical information. Hindenburg disaster, shooting of Oswald, nomination of Jimmy
Carter, etc. 160pp. 8¼ x 11.
23667-6 Pa. $5.00

THE ART OF THE CINEMATOGRAPHER, Leonard Maltin. Survey of
American cinematography history and anecdotal interviews with 5 masters—
Arthur Miller, Hal Mohr, Hal Rosson, Lucien Ballard, and Conrad Hall.
Very large selection of behind-the-scenes production photos. 105 photographs. Filmographies. Index. Originally Behind the Camera. 144pp.
8¼ x 11.
23686-2 Pa. $5.00

DESIGNS FOR THE THREE-CORNERED HAT (LE TRICORNE),
Pablo Picasso. 32 fabulously rare drawings—including 31 color illustrations
of costumes and accessories—for 1919 production of famous ballet. Edited
by Parmenia Migel, who has written new introduction. 48pp. 9⅜ x 12¼.
(Available in U.S. only)
23709-5 Pa. $5.00

NOTES OF A FILM DIRECTOR, Sergei Eisenstein. Greatest Russian
filmmaker explains montage, making of Alexander Nevsky, aesthetics; comments on self, associates, great rivals (Chaplin), similar material. 78 illustrations. 240pp. 5⅜ x 8½.
22392-2 Pa. $4.50

HOLLYWOOD GLAMOUR PORTRAITS, edited by John Kobal. 145 photos capture the stars from 1926-49, the high point in portrait photography. Gable, Harlow, Bogart, Bacall, Hedy Lamarr, Marlene Dietrich, Robert Montgomery, Marlon Brando, Veronica Lake; 94 stars in all. Full background on photographers, technical aspects, much more. Total of 160pp. 8⅜ x 11¼. 23352-9 Pa. $5.00

THE NEW YORK STAGE: FAMOUS PRODUCTIONS IN PHOTO-GRAPHS, edited by Stanley Appelbaum. 148 photographs from Museum of City of New York show 142 plays, 1883-1939. *Peter Pan, The Front Page, Dead End, Our Town*, O'Neill, hundreds of actors and actresses, etc. Full indexes. 154pp. 9½ x 10. 23241-7 Pa. $6.00

MASTERS OF THE DRAMA, John Gassner. Most comprehensive history of the drama, every tradition from Greeks to modern Europe and America, including Orient. Covers 800 dramatists, 2000 plays; biography, plot summaries, criticism, theatre history, etc. 77 illustrations. 890pp. 5⅜ x 8½. 20100-7 Clothbd. $10.00

THE GREAT OPERA STARS IN HISTORIC PHOTOGRAPHS, edited by James Camner. 343 portraits from the 1850s to the 1940s: Tamburini, Mario, Caliapin, Jeritza, Melchior, Melba, Patti, Pinza, Schipa, Caruso, Farrar, Steber, Gobbi, and many more—270 performers in all. Index. 199pp. 8⅜ x 11¼. 23575-0 Pa. $6.50

J. S. BACH, Albert Schweitzer. Great full-length study of Bach, life, background to music, music, by foremost modern scholar. Ernest Newman translation. 650 musical examples. Total of 928pp. 5⅜ x 8½. (Available in U.S. only) 21631-4, 21632-2 Pa., Two-vol. set $10.00

COMPLETE PIANO SONATAS, Ludwig van Beethoven. All sonatas in the fine Schenker edition, with fingering, analytical material. One of best modern editions. Total of 615pp. 9 x 12. (Available in U.S. only) 23134-8, 23135-6 Pa., Two-vol. set $15.00

KEYBOARD MUSIC, J. S. Bach. Bach-Gesellschaft edition. For harpsichord, piano, other keyboard instruments. English Suites, French Suites, Six Partitas, Goldberg Variations, Two-Part Inventions, Three-Part Sinfonias. 312pp. 8⅛ x 11. (Available in U.S. only) 22360-4 Pa. $6.00

FOUR SYMPHONIES IN FULL SCORE, Franz Schubert. Schubert's four most popular symphonies: No. 4 in C Minor ("Tragic"); No. 5 in B-flat Major; No. 8 in B Minor ("Unfinished"); No. 9 in C Major ("Great"). Breitkopf & Hartel edition. Study score. 261pp. 9⅜ x 12¼. 23681-1 Pa. $6.50

THE AUTHENTIC GILBERT & SULLIVAN SONGBOOK, W. S. Gilbert, A. S. Sullivan. Largest selection available; 92 songs, uncut, original keys, in piano rendering approved by Sullivan. Favorites and lesser-known fine numbers. Edited with plot synopses by James Spero. 3 illustrations. 399pp. 9 x 12. 23482-7 Pa. $7.95

PRINCIPLES OF ORCHESTRATION, Nikolay Rimsky-Korsakov. Great classical orchestrator provides fundamentals of tonal resonance, progression of parts, voice and orchestra, tutti effects, much else in major document. 330pp. of musical excerpts. 489pp. 6½ x 9¼. 21266-1 Pa. $6.00

TRISTAN UND ISOLDE, Richard Wagner. Full orchestral score with complete instrumentation. Do not confuse with piano reduction. Commentary by Felix Mottl, great Wagnerian conductor and scholar. Study score. 655pp. 8⅛ x 11. 22915-7 Pa. $12.50

REQUIEM IN FULL SCORE, Giuseppe Verdi. Immensely popular with choral groups and music lovers. Republication of edition published by C. F. Peters, Leipzig, n. d. German frontmaker in English translation. Glossary. Text in Latin. Study score. 204pp. 9⅜ x 12¼.
23682-X Pa. $6.00

COMPLETE CHAMBER MUSIC FOR STRINGS, Felix Mendelssohn. All of Mendelssohn's chamber music: Octet, 2 Quintets, 6 Quartets, and Four Pieces for String Quartet. (Nothing with piano is included). Complete works edition (1874-7). Study score. 283 pp. 9⅜ x 12¼.
23679-X Pa. $6.95

POPULAR SONGS OF NINETEENTH-CENTURY AMERICA, edited by Richard Jackson. 64 most important songs: "Old Oaken Bucket," "Arkansas Traveler," "Yellow Rose of Texas," etc. Authentic original sheet music, full introduction and commentaries. 290pp. 9 x 12. 23270-0 Pa. $6.00

COLLECTED PIANO WORKS, Scott Joplin. Edited by Vera Brodsky Lawrence. Practically all of Joplin's piano works—rags, two-steps, marches, waltzes, etc., 51 works in all. Extensive introduction by Rudi Blesh. Total of 345pp. 9 x 12. 23106-2 Pa. $14.95

BASIC PRINCIPLES OF CLASSICAL BALLET, Agrippina Vaganova. Great Russian theoretician, teacher explains methods for teaching classical ballet; incorporates best from French, Italian, Russian schools. 118 illustrations. 175pp. 5⅜ x 8½. 22036-2 Pa. $2.50

CHINESE CHARACTERS, L. Wieger. Rich analysis of 2300 characters according to traditional systems into primitives. Historical-semantic analysis to phonetics (Classical Mandarin) and radicals. 820pp. 6⅛ x 9¼.
21321-8 Pa. $10.00

EGYPTIAN LANGUAGE: EASY LESSONS IN EGYPTIAN HIERO-GLYPHICS, E. A. Wallis Budge. Foremost Egyptologist offers Egyptian grammar, explanation of hieroglyphics, many reading texts, dictionary of symbols. 246pp. 5 x 7½. (Available in U.S. only)
21394-3 Clothbd. $7.50

AN ETYMOLOGICAL DICTIONARY OF MODERN ENGLISH, Ernest Weekley. Richest, fullest work, by foremost British lexicographer. Detailed word histories. Inexhaustible. Do not confuse this with Concise Etymological Dictionary, which is abridged. Total of 856pp. 6½ x 9¼.
21873-2, 21874-0 Pa., Two-vol. set $12.00

A MAYA GRAMMAR, Alfred M. Tozzer. Practical, useful English-language grammar by the Harvard anthropologist who was one of the three greatest American scholars in the area of Maya culture. Phonetics, grammatical processes, syntax, more. 301pp. 5⅜ x 8½.   23465-7 Pa. $4.00

THE JOURNAL OF HENRY D. THOREAU, edited by Bradford Torrey, F. H. Allen. Complete reprinting of 14 volumes, 1837-61, over two million words; the sourcebooks for *Walden*, etc. Definitive. All original sketches, plus 75 photographs. Introduction by Walter Harding. Total of 1804pp. 8½ x 12¼.   20312-3, 20313-1 Clothbd., Two-vol. set $50.00

CLASSIC GHOST STORIES, Charles Dickens and others. 18 wonderful stories you've wanted to reread: "The Monkey's Paw," "The House and the Brain," "The Upper Berth," "The Signalman," "Dracula's Guest," "The Tapestried Chamber," etc. Dickens, Scott, Mary Shelley, Stoker, etc. 330pp. 5⅜ x 8½.   20735-8 Pa. $3.50

SEVEN SCIENCE FICTION NOVELS, H. G. Wells. Full novels. *First Men in the Moon, Island of Dr. Moreau, War of the Worlds, Food of the Gods, Invisible Man, Time Machine, In the Days of the Comet.* A basic science-fiction library. 1015pp. 5⅜ x 8½. (Available in U.S. only)   20264-X Clothbd. $8.95

ARMADALE, Wilkie Collins. Third great mystery novel by the author of *The Woman in White* and *The Moonstone*. Ingeniously plotted narrative shows an exceptional command of character, incident and mood. Original magazine version with 40 illustrations. 597pp. 5⅜ x 8½.   23429-0 Pa. $5.00

MASTERS OF MYSTERY, H. Douglas Thomson. The first book in English (1931) devoted to history and aesthetics of detective story. Poe, Doyle, LeFanu, Dickens, many others, up to 1930. New introduction and notes by E. F. Bleiler. 288pp. 5⅜ x 8½. (Available in U.S. only)   23606-4 Pa. $4.00

FLATLAND, E. A. Abbott. Science-fiction classic explores life of 2-D being in 3-D world. Read also as introduction to thought about hyperspace. Introduction by Banesh Hoffmann. 16 illustrations. 103pp. 5⅜ x 8½.   20001-9 Pa. $1.75

THREE SUPERNATURAL NOVELS OF THE VICTORIAN PERIOD, edited, with an introduction, by E. F. Bleiler. Reprinted complete and unabridged, three great classics of the supernatural: *The Haunted Hotel* by Wilkie Collins, *The Haunted House at Latchford* by Mrs. J. H. Riddell, and *The Lost Stradivarius* by J. Meade Falkner. 325pp. 5⅜ x 8½.   22571-2 Pa. $4.00

AYESHA: THE RETURN OF "SHE," H. Rider Haggard. Virtuoso sequel featuring the great mythic creation, Ayesha, in an adventure that is fully as good as the first book, *She*. Original magazine version, with 47 original illustrations by Maurice Greiffenhagen. 189pp. 6½ x 9¼.   23649-8 Pa. $3.50

UNCLE SILAS, J. Sheridan LeFanu. Victorian Gothic mystery novel, considered by many best of period, even better than Collins or Dickens. Wonderful psychological terror. Introduction by Frederick Shroyer. 436pp. 5⅜ x 8½. 21715-9 Pa. $6.00

JURGEN, James Branch Cabell. The great erotic fantasy of the 1920's that delighted thousands, shocked thousands more. Full final text, Lane edition with 13 plates by Frank Pape. 346pp. 5⅜ x 8½.
23507-6 Pa. $4.50

THE CLAVERINGS, Anthony Trollope. Major novel, chronicling aspects of British Victorian society, personalities. Reprint of Cornhill serialization, 16 plates by M. Edwards; first reprint of full text. Introduction by Norman Donaldson. 412pp. 5⅜ x 8½. 23464-9 Pa. $5.00

KEPT IN THE DARK, Anthony Trollope. Unusual short novel about Victorian morality and abnormal psychology by the great English author. Probably the first American publication. Frontispiece by Sir John Millais. 92pp. 6½ x 9¼. 23609-9 Pa. $2.50

RALPH THE HEIR, Anthony Trollope. Forgotten tale of illegitimacy, inheritance. Master novel of Trollope's later years. Victorian country estates, clubs, Parliament, fox hunting, world of fully realized characters. Reprint of 1871 edition. 12 illustrations by F. A. Faser. 434pp. of text. 5⅜ x 8½. 23642-0 Pa. $5.00

YEKL and THE IMPORTED BRIDEGROOM AND OTHER STORIES OF THE NEW YORK GHETTO, Abraham Cahan. Film *Hester Street* based on *Yekl* (1896). Novel, other stories among first about Jewish immigrants of N.Y.'s East Side. Highly praised by W. D. Howells—Cahan "a new star of realism." New introduction by Bernard G. Richards. 240pp. 5⅜ x 8½. 22427-9 Pa. $3.50

THE HIGH PLACE, James Branch Cabell. Great fantasy writer's enchanting comedy of disenchantment set in 18th-century France. Considered by some critics to be even better than his famous *Jurgen*. 10 illustrations and numerous vignettes by noted fantasy artist Frank C. Pape. 320pp. 5⅜ x 8½. 23670-6 Pa. $4.00

ALICE'S ADVENTURES UNDER GROUND, Lewis Carroll. Facsimile of ms. Carroll gave Alice Liddell in 1864. Different in many ways from final Alice. Handlettered, illustrated by Carroll. Introduction by Martin Gardner. 128pp. 5⅜ x 8½. 21482-6 Pa. $2.00

FAVORITE ANDREW LANG FAIRY TALE BOOKS IN MANY COLORS, Andrew Lang. The four Lang favorites in a boxed set—the complete *Red, Green, Yellow* and *Blue* Fairy Books. 164 stories; 439 illustrations by Lancelot Speed, Henry Ford and G. P. Jacomb Hood. Total of about 1500pp. 5⅜ x 8½. 23407-X Boxed set, Pa. $14.95

HOUSEHOLD STORIES BY THE BROTHERS GRIMM. All the great Grimm stories: "Rumpelstiltskin," "Snow White," "Hansel and Gretel," etc., with 114 illustrations by Walter Crane. 269pp. 5⅜ x 8½.
21080-4 Pa. $3.00

SLEEPING BEAUTY, illustrated by Arthur Rackham. Perhaps the fullest, most delightful version ever, told by C. S. Evans. Rackham's best work. 49 illustrations. 110pp. 7⅞ x 10¾.   22756-1 Pa. $2.50

AMERICAN FAIRY TALES, L. Frank Baum. Young cowboy lassoes Father Time; dummy in Mr. Floman's department store window comes to life; and 10 other fairy tales. 41 illustrations by N. P. Hall, Harry Kennedy, Ike Morgan, and Ralph Gardner. 209pp. 5⅜ x 8½.   23643-9 Pa. $3.00

THE WONDERFUL WIZARD OF OZ, L. Frank Baum. Facsimile in full color of America's finest children's classic. Introduction by Martin Gardner. 143 illustrations by W. W. Denslow. 267pp. 5⅜ x 8½.
20691-2 Pa. $3.50

THE TALE OF PETER RABBIT, Beatrix Potter. The inimitable Peter's terrifying adventure in Mr. McGregor's garden, with all 27 wonderful, full-color Potter illustrations. 55pp. 4¼ x 5½. (Available in U.S. only)
22827-4 Pa. $1.25

THE STORY OF KING ARTHUR AND HIS KNIGHTS, Howard Pyle. Finest children's version of life of King Arthur. 48 illustrations by Pyle. 131pp. 6⅛ x 9¼.   21445-1 Pa. $4.95

CARUSO'S CARICATURES, Enrico Caruso. Great tenor's remarkable caricatures of self, fellow musicians, composers, others. Toscanini, Puccini, Farrar, etc. Impish, cutting, insightful. 473 illustrations. Preface by M. Sisca. 217pp. 8⅜ x 11¼.   23528-9 Pa. $6.95

PERSONAL NARRATIVE OF A PILGRIMAGE TO ALMADINAH AND MECCAH, Richard Burton. Great travel classic by remarkably colorful personality. Burton, disguised as a Moroccan, visited sacred shrines of Islam, narrowly escaping death. Wonderful observations of Islamic life, customs, personalities. 47 illustrations. Total of 959pp. 5⅜ x 8½.
21217-3, 21218-1 Pa., Two-vol. set $12.00

INCIDENTS OF TRAVEL IN YUCATAN, John L. Stephens. Classic (1843) exploration of jungles of Yucatan, looking for evidences of Maya civilization. Travel adventures, Mexican and Indian culture, etc. Total of 669pp. 5⅜ x 8½.   20926-1, 20927-X Pa., Two-vol. set $7.90

AMERICAN LITERARY AUTOGRAPHS FROM WASHINGTON IRVING TO HENRY JAMES, Herbert Cahoon, et al. Letters, poems, manuscripts of Hawthorne, Thoreau, Twain, Alcott, Whitman, 67 other prominent American authors. Reproductions, full transcripts and commentary. Plus checklist of all American Literary Autographs in The Pierpont Morgan Library. Printed on exceptionally high-quality paper. 136 illustrations. 212pp. 9⅛ x 12¼.   23548-3 Pa. $7.95

YUCATAN BEFORE AND AFTER THE CONQUEST, Diego de Landa. First English translation of basic book in Maya studies, the only significant account of Yucatan written in the early post-Conquest era. Translated by distinguished Maya scholar William Gates. Appendices, introduction, 4 maps and over 120 illustrations added by translator. 162pp. 5⅜ x 8½.
23622-6 Pa. $3.00

THE MALAY ARCHIPELAGO, Alfred R. Wallace. Spirited travel account by one of founders of modern biology. Touches on zoology, botany, ethnography, geography, and geology. 62 illustrations, maps. 515pp. 5⅜ x 8½.
20187-2 Pa. $6.95

THE DISCOVERY OF THE TOMB OF TUTANKHAMEN, Howard Carter, A. C. Mace. Accompany Carter in the thrill of discovery, as ruined passage suddenly reveals unique, untouched, fabulously rich tomb. Fascinating account, with 106 illustrations. New introduction by J. M. White. Total of 382pp. 5⅜ x 8½. (Available in U.S. only)   23500-9 Pa. $4.00

THE WORLD'S GREATEST SPEECHES, edited by Lewis Copeland and Lawrence W. Lamm. Vast collection of 278 speeches from Greeks up to present. Powerful and effective models; unique look at history. Revised to 1970. Indices. 842pp. 5⅜ x 8½.   20468-5 Pa. $8.95

THE 100 GREATEST ADVERTISEMENTS, Julian Watkins. The priceless ingredient; His master's voice; 99 44/100% pure; over 100 others. How they were written, their impact, etc. Remarkable record. 130 illustrations. 233pp. 7⅞ x 10 3/5.   20540-1 Pa. $5.00

CRUICKSHANK PRINTS FOR HAND COLORING, George Cruickshank. 18 illustrations, one side of a page, on fine-quality paper suitable for watercolors. Caricatures of people in society (c. 1820) full of trenchant wit. Very large format. 32pp. 11 x 16.   23684-6 Pa. $5.00

THIRTY-TWO COLOR POSTCARDS OF TWENTIETH-CENTURY AMERICAN ART, Whitney Museum of American Art. Reproduced in full color in postcard form are 31 art works and one shot of the museum. Calder, Hopper, Rauschenberg, others. Detachable. 16pp. 8¼ x 11.
23629-3 Pa. $2.50

MUSIC OF THE SPHERES: THE MATERIAL UNIVERSE FROM ATOM TO QUASAR SIMPLY EXPLAINED, Guy Murchie. Planets, stars, geology, atoms, radiation, relativity, quantum theory, light, antimatter, similar topics. 319 figures. 664pp. 5⅜ x 8½.
21809-0, 21810-4 Pa., Two-vol. set $10.00

EINSTEIN'S THEORY OF RELATIVITY, Max Born. Finest semi-technical account; covers Einstein, Lorentz, Minkowski, and others, with much detail, much explanation of ideas and math not readily available elsewhere on this level. For student, non-specialist. 376pp. 5⅜ x 8½.
60769-0 Pa. $4.50

AMERICAN ANTIQUE FURNITURE, Edgar G. Miller, Jr. The basic coverage of all American furniture before 1840: chapters per item chronologically cover all types of furniture, with more than 2100 photos. Total of 1106pp. 7⅞ x 10¾.   21599-7, 21600-4 Pa., Two-vol. set $17.90

ILLUSTRATED GUIDE TO SHAKER FURNITURE, Robert Meader. Director, Shaker Museum, Old Chatham, presents up-to-date coverage of all furniture and appurtenances, with much on local styles not available elsewhere. 235 photos. 146pp. 9 x 12.   22819-3 Pa. $5.00

ORIENTAL RUGS, ANTIQUE AND MODERN, Walter A. Hawley. Persia, Turkey, Caucasus, Central Asia, China, other traditions. Best general survey of all aspects: styles and periods, manufacture, uses, symbols and their interpretation, and identification. 96 illustrations, 11 in color. 320pp. 6⅛ x 9¼.   22366-3 Pa. $6.95

CHINESE POTTERY AND PORCELAIN, R. L. Hobson. Detailed descriptions and analyses by former Keeper of the Department of Oriental Antiquities and Ethnography at the British Museum. Covers hundreds of pieces from primitive times to 1915. Still the standard text for most periods. 136 plates, 40 in full color. Total of 750pp. 5⅜ x 8½.
23253-0 Pa. $10.00

THE WARES OF THE MING DYNASTY, R. L. Hobson. Foremost scholar examines and illustrates many varieties of Ming (1368-1644). Famous blue and white, polychrome, lesser-known styles and shapes. 117 illustrations, 9 full color, of outstanding pieces. Total of 263pp. 6⅛ x 9¼. (Available in U.S. only)   23652-8 Pa. $6.00